The woman wit[h] ... [pro]wl as a point of c[ontact] ... [Rab]bi Kluge unlocks the mysteries of the tallit to be your point of contact with the supernatural!

—SID ROTH
HOST, *IT'S SUPERNATURAL!*

As a Jewish believer and leader in the Messianic Jewish movement for over thirty years, my dear friend Rabbi Kluge shares a wealth of knowledge from his upbringing, training, and experience. This is a unique book that will provide rich insight on the prayer shawl that will deepen your prayer life and intimacy with God.

—RABBI JONATHAN BERNIS
PRESIDENT AND CEO, JEWISH VOICE
MINISTRIES INTERNATIONAL

Dr. Kluge's book teaches us about one of the holiest objects of Judaism, the tallit (prayer shawl). We learn its traditional meaning and then about its pathway to God's presence, healing, love, forgiveness, and other hidden treasures. I have experienced firsthand the work of Dr. Kluge's important ministry and highly recommend the reading of this excellent book.

—JAMES L. GARLOW
SENIOR PASTOR, SKYLINE CHURCH, SAN DIEGO, CALIFORNIA
NEW YORK TIMES BEST-SELLING AUTHOR,
CRACKING DA VINCI'S CODE

Messianic Rabbi Charles Kluge offers a rich, scriptural meditation on the beauty and power of the tallit, the traditional Jewish prayer shawl. Your heart will be stirred for deeper intimacy with God as you read these inspiring words.

—Dr. Michael L. Brown
Author, *The Real Kosher Jesus*

The tallit, so precious in the life and ministry of the Messianic Jewish community, is largely mystery to the non-Jewish body of Messiah. This book removes the mystery and provides compelling insight and understanding of the power, presence, and intimate blessing that can be discovered in the tallit. This book is a must-read for all, especially we Gentiles, because we have equal opportunity to receive Yeshua's blessings through the tallit.

—Dr. Raleigh Washington
President and CEO, Promise Keepers

Dr. Kluge has taken on a great challenge by writing such an in-depth book about the tallit and its connection with the Jewish roots of our faith, both for Jews and Gentiles. He has explained with a deep conviction and passion about the wonders of the tallit, and he has approached this subject sensibly and with great sensitivity. We understand that the tallit is a revered and respected material object, however, we are led back to the knowledge of our relationship that all things are wrapped around by the love of Yeshua the Messiah. This is the most informative and balanced book I have read about the tallit.

—Barry Segal
President, Vision for Israel

Dr. Kluge's new book, *The Tallit*, helps a person who is not familiar with Jewish tradition appreciate this holy object that symbolizes the relationship of devout men and women to the Word of God and also sheds light on the faithfulness of God to those men and women who revere His Word. Rabbi Kluge helps us discover that there are experiences with God that are hidden from the casual observer. While teaching the traditions connected with the wearing of the tallit, Rabbi Kluge takes us on a journey that can help us experience the supernatural by bringing us into a greater intimacy with God and His Word.

—Michaelis J. Gonzalez
General Manager, WFGC Television/
Christian Television Network

Over the years people have asked me, "What is that thing you're wearing?" They were referring to my tallit. From now on I can answer their questions by referring them to *The Tallit: Experiencing the Mystery of the Prayer Shawl and Other Hidden Treasures* by Rabbi Charlie Kluge. This unique work binds Scripture, tradition, history, and anecdote together to help express the essence of the tallit as beautifully as the tying of the *tzitzit* together helps express the essence of Hashem.

—Rabbi Eric Tokajer
Author and Publisher, *The Messianic Times*

This book explains the why, where, when, and how of the tallit both from the Bible and from Jewish tradition. It also contains a carefully woven story of a man and the challenges and victories of his life of faith. First a politically motivated optometrist, he eventually became the president of the Messianic Jewish Alliance. All along the way he was a peacemaker and a bridge builder. Enjoy!

—DR. NEIL LASH
PRESIDENT, JEWISH JEWELS

THE
TALLIT

THE
TALLIT

CHARLIE
KLUGE

CHARISMA
HOUSE

Most CHARISMA HOUSE BOOK GROUP products are available at special quantity discounts for bulk purchase for sales promotions, premiums, fund-raising, and educational needs. For details, write Charisma House Book Group, 600 Rinehart Road, Lake Mary, Florida 32746, or telephone (407) 333-0600.

THE TALLIT by Charlie Kluge
Published by Charisma House
Charisma Media/Charisma House Book Group
600 Rinehart Road
Lake Mary, Florida 32746
www.charismahouse.com

Cover design by Justin Evans

Visit the author's website at www.gesherinternational.com.

Library of Congress Cataloging-in-Publication Data:
Names: Kluge, Charlie, author.
Title: The tallit / Charlie Kluge.
Description: Lake Mary, Florida : Charisma House, 2016. |
Includes bibliographical references and index.
Identifiers: LCCN 2016032361| ISBN 9781629987330 (trade
paper : alk. paper) | ISBN 9781629987347 (ebook)
Subjects: LCSH: Tallitot (Jewish liturgical objects) |
Christianity and other religions--Judaism. | Judaism--
Relations--Christianity. | Jewish Christians.
Classification: LCC BM657.T35 K58 2016 | DDC
296.4/61--dc23
LC record available at https://lccn.loc.gov/2016032361

Some names and identifying details of people in this book
have been changed to protect the privacy of those individuals.

While the author has made every effort to provide accurate
Internet addresses at the time of publication, neither the
publisher nor the author assumes any responsibility for errors
or for changes that occur after publication.

16 17 18 19 20 — 9 8 7 6 5 4 3 2
Printed in the United States of America

CONTENTS

ACKNOWLEDGMENTS

WITH MUCH APPRECIATION and gratitude, I would like to thank all of the people who have diligently worked with me from the beginning of this project to its conclusion.

Thank you to my absolutely wonderful and beautiful wife, Racquel, for your complete love, dedication, encouragement, and steadfast determination in helping me to stay on schedule.

Thank you to Joan Bullock for your help and wisdom so I could move forward with this project.

Thank you to Steve Strang for your obedience to the *Ruach HaKodesh* (Holy Spirit).

Thank you to my editors, Debbie Marrie and Adrienne Gaines, for your patience and discernment from start to finish. Thank you also to Ann Mulchan and Althea Thompson from Charisma House for your help with this project.

Most of all, thank you to "the Teacher," Yeshua *HaMashiach*, for giving me life, redemption, divine inspiration, and eternal love.

PREFACE

I T WAS THE end of January 2015, and our congregation was about two or three days from ending our three-week fast. I believed that God put on my heart to write a book, but I knew undertaking a writing project would take a very concentrated and extensive amount of time. Should I start to write or not? "Oh, Lord," I prayed, "If this is really You putting it on my heart that it's time to write a book, I need a sign from You."

About three days later, I received a phone call from Steve Strang, a friend and the publisher of Charisma House. He told me that he wanted to ask me a strange question. I replied, "OK, go ahead." He went on to tell me that about two or three days before, God had put my name on his mind and heart, and he wanted to discuss a book project with me.

That conversation was the beginning of the book you hold in your hands. I believe God's hand has been on this project from start to finish, and I believe His purpose is to use it to deepen your walk with Him as you understand the spiritual treasure that is the tallit. This book is a supernatural answer to prayer, and my prayer for you now is that God would use what is written in these pages to draw you closer to Himself and speak to your heart.

INTRODUCTION

I T WAS A beautiful summer day in early August of 1963. I was almost fourteen and sitting at the top of the stairs on the porch of my cabin at Camp Delmont. The eight-week summer camp was held in Livingston Manor, New York, which is a beautiful small town in the Catskill Mountains. As I sat there with my friends, who were already fourteen, we began to talk about how lucky we were. We were on the top of the world because everything we had was "the best." We lived in New York State, which was the best state. We lived in New York City, which was the best city. We lived in Queens, which was the best borough. I lived in Bayside, which was the best town in Queens. I was a Yankees fan, which was the best team with the best players.

That was my sixth summer at Delmont, and I went for three more years, but for some reason I've always remembered that conversation with my friends in 1963. It was one of the reasons I began searching to find out what life was all about when I was in college. I wanted "the best" life possible, and I felt God must somehow be part of experiencing that. In His perfect timing, God used that journey to reveal Himself to me. Since then, as I have sought to understand the mysteries of God, He has revealed several hidden treasures that help us come to know Him more intimately here on this earth. One of those treasures is the tallit (טלית).

While the tallit is a physical garment that is used in many Jewish traditions and throughout a person's life cycle, it also has a rich spiritual dimension. In this book we will study these spiritual meanings of the Jewish prayer shawl. The tallit reminds us of God's presence, power, protection, covering, healing, and love. In it we also see the latter-day prophetic revelations of Moses and the Hebrew prophets fulfilled.

Most importantly, in these pages we will discover how the tallit points us to the Messiah of Israel: Yeshua *Mishikeinu* (Jesus our Messiah). He is the one of whom Moshe *Rabbeinu* (Moses our Teacher) spoke when he said, "ADONAI your God will raise up for you a prophet like me from your midst—from your brothers. To him you must listen" (Deut. 18:15). Because of Yeshua, Jew and Gentile have become "one new man," which means the tallit can be used by anyone who chooses to follow the Word of God. Therefore, we must listen to the words of both Moshe *Rabbeinu* and Yeshua *Rabbeinu* (Yeshua our Teacher). It is Yeshua "the Teacher" who places deep inside of us, in our *kishkes* ("deep insides"), the revelation of these hidden treasures.

That is what happened to me. I was given my first tallit almost fifty-four years ago at my bar mitzvah. But it wasn't until I embraced Yeshua as my Messiah that I discovered the true intimacy we can have with God when we come under the tallit in prayer. All my life, God had been dropping what I call "love notes" to me, but I didn't understand them until I chose to follow His course for my life. I was raised to respect and honor *Hashem* (the Name, God), and when I was just five years old my father taught me to pray the Shema (which begins, "Hear, O Israel, the LORD is our God, the LORD is One") every night before I went to sleep. But "Jesus" was not a name we uttered in my home.

Despite my observant Jewish upbringing, I found myself wanting to know God intimately, to understand the purpose for our existence. In college, I explored different beliefs, but that didn't fill the longing I had. After I graduated, I became a pediatric optometrist with a busy practice, but I was still searching. Thankfully, God led me to friends who not only prayed for me, but also showed me what it was like to have a relationship with Messiah. In time, my wife, Racquel, and I came to embrace Yeshua not as *a* Messiah or *a* Lamb of God but as *the* Messiah, *the* Lamb of God.

Knowing Yeshua turned our lives upside down. I developed an insatiable appetite to understand His Word. I studied rabbinic and Christian commentaries as well as the Jewish writings of antiquity, which only made me more convinced that Yeshua was truly the Messiah. Because of my passion for God and His Word, I retired from my medical practice to concentrate on ministry, and soon God opened doors for me to become a Messianic rabbi and lead a congregation of believers in Yeshua, which I still do to this day. (To read my full testimony, please see the appendix.)

Understanding the heart of Yeshua has shed new light on the purpose and spiritual significance of the tallit. In Jewish culture it is used in all the major life-cycle events and represents a journey from birth to death. But when my spiritual eyes were opened to Messiah, I began to see how Yeshua revealed Himself through the tallit and why knowing its symbolism helps many people draw closer to Him. That is my purpose for writing this book—to share with you the spiritual treasures hidden within the Jewish prayer shawl. And because I want to make this information as accessible as I can, I have included a glossary at the end of the book to define the many Hebrew words I use. It is my prayer that understanding these mysteries will help you deepen your intimacy with Hashem and understand more fully the love God has for us, His children.

Having said that, I want to issue a word of caution. The tallit is a holy object given to us by God, and we show Him honor and respect in the way we use it. Yet there is nothing mystical or kabbalistic about the tallit. It should not be considered a prescription for holiness and righteousness or something that is used to effect miracles, signs, and wonders. That can transpire only as a direct consequence of the perfect will of God.

However, the tallit can help us experience the supernatural by bringing us into a greater intimacy with God and His Word. The tzitzit sewn on each of the four corners of the garment remind us of the Word of God, and when we come under the tallit in prayer, we are able to block out distractions and focus on Hashem (the Name, God). That is why for the last 3,500 years great servants of the Lord who have followed the teachings of Moshe Rabbeinu and/or Yeshua Mishikeinu have experienced miracles while being wrapped in the tallit.

Miracles are still occurring as we seek Hashem under the tallit. I believe that, as you read about the mysteries of the prayer shawl, Adonai will give you "treasures of darkness and hidden riches of secret places" (Isa. 45:3) so that you may truly become intimate with the Shepherd of Israel and, in His presence under the tallit, receive His blessings of healing, love, and forgiveness.

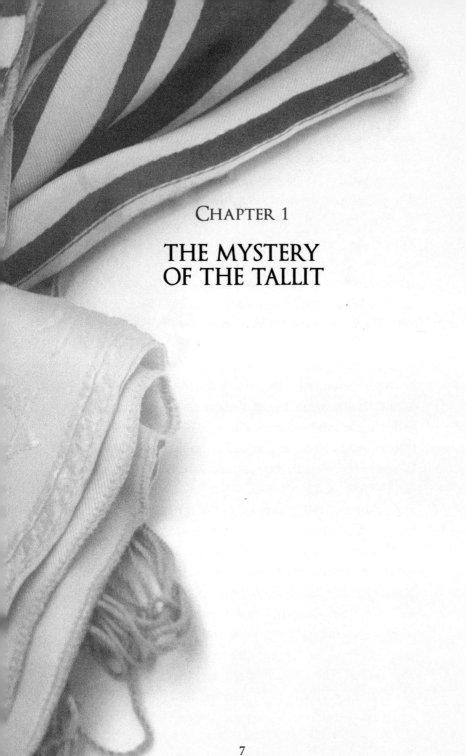

CHAPTER 1

THE MYSTERY OF THE TALLIT

M ORE AND MORE, as I travel to speak in churches, I meet people who are seeking to understand the Jewish roots of the Christian faith. They will blow the shofar, pray the Shema, and don a tallit during prayer. At the synagogue I lead, we keep tallitot (the plural form of *tallit*) for guests to use during the service, and many are eager to do so. Coming under the tallit often helps a person seek Yeshua without distraction and commune with the *Ruach HaKodesh* (Holy Spirit) in a whole new way. I have heard many people say that coming under a tallit in prayer helped them deepen their intimacy with Hashem. The tallit does not have special power in itself, but it reminds us of God and His Word, in which we find all power.

We experienced this vividly during a recent service at the congregation I lead, Gesher Shalom. It was a Saturday night, and we were meeting for the Erev Shavuot (the evening of Shavuot, which is known as the Feast of Weeks or Pentecost). Shavuot occurs on the sixth day of the Hebrew month of Sivan, which falls between mid-May and mid-June, and it commemorates the day God revealed the Torah to the nation of Israel on Mount Sinai.

The service began with over an hour of prayer during which we welcomed the presence of Adonai and the outpouring of His Ruach HaKodesh. After our time of prayer, we read from Scripture and I gave a short *d'rash*, or sermon, but the Holy Spirit was moving in such a way that we spent most of the evening in praise, worship, dance, and prayer. The service lasted for about six-and-a-half hours and could have continued for more.

During that time, we felt the presence of the Ruach in

a most powerful way. I sensed a leading to call those who wanted to rededicate their lives to the Teacher, Yeshua HaMashiach, to come forward and stand under the tallit. Over one hundred people responded to the call. We prayed, among other things, for deeper revelations of His Word, breakthroughs, and special protection for family members.

One woman who came forward prayed for her son's protection. Little did we know, he and his friends had decided to visit the Pulse nightclub in downtown Orlando, Florida, but when he stepped inside, the young man felt he should leave, so he did. Later that night a gunman entered the club and opened fire, killing forty-nine people and injuring dozens more.

After receiving prayer under the tallit that night, a seven-year-old boy broke down and cried for a long time. The Ruach fell upon him in such a powerful way that he was able to release his hurts to the Lord. A fourteen-year-old boy who also came and stood under the tallit asked his mother, "What is this different feeling I am experiencing?" She told him it was the infilling of the Ruach HaKodesh, and after that night his desire to serve Yeshua intensified. One woman who had been in pain for several years and couldn't sit for more than five minutes told me she had been able to sit for more than two hours that night and experienced no pain.

The breakthroughs and testimonies from that prayer meeting are still coming in to us. Prayer under the tallit can bring powerful results when the *dunamis* (dynamite-like) power of God is present! As we came under the tallit that night, we were reminded of the holiness of God, His

Word, and His power, and we experienced His presence in a dynamic way. So if praying under the tallit can have this kind of impact, you may be wondering, "What exactly is a tallit and what makes it so special?"

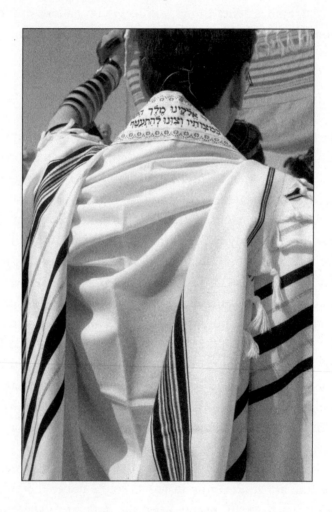

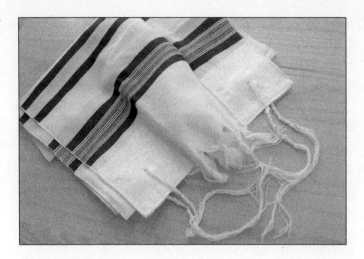

The tallit is the Jewish prayer shawl. It is rectangular and generally white with blue or black stripes, and it has tassels on each of its four corners called tzitzit. The tallit can be large (tallit *gadol*) and cover a person's entire body, or it can be small (tallit *katan*). But it must be long enough to be worn over the shoulders as a shawl and not just around the neck as a scarf. Men often wear a tallit katan under their shirts with the tzitzit left hanging out so they can look at the tzitzit all day long and remember God's commands. A person wearing a tallit gadol will generally keep it draped over his shoulders, but during times of prayer he will use it to cover his head.

Traditionally men have worn the prayer shawl because Jewish law did not obligate women to wear them and the Torah discourages women from wearing men's garments. But now there are many styles and colors available that are very feminine, so both men and women wear tallitot. Although the stripes on the tallit are usually navy or black, they also can be any color of the rainbow. The tallit is classically made of wool, cotton, or silk, but it can be made out of any material so long as the prohibition against combining linen and wool is observed.

As I mentioned previously, for a Jewish person the tallit is typically used in every major life-cycle event—from circumcision to bar/bat mitzvah to marriage and even death. But it is most frequently used in prayer. Tallitot are generally worn at morning Shabbat services and during morning prayers. An exception is the Kol Nidre, the evening service on the eve of Yom Kippur (Day of Atonement), during which the tallit is also worn.

Yom Kippur is considered the holiest day of the Jewish year, a Sabbath of Sabbaths observed on the tenth day of the Hebrew month of Tishri, which falls in September or early October. All work is suspended and observers fast for twenty-five hours, beginning before sunset the evening before Yom Kippur and ending after nightfall on Yom Kippur. It is a time when we "afflict the soul" and atone for sins committed and promises broken to God and between people.

The tallit is worn during the first evening service of Yom Kippur, Kol Nidre, which would traditionally begin before sunset. This is significant because, according to Jewish tradition, the tallit was to be worn only during the daylight. This is because the purpose of the tallit is to see the tzitzit and remember God's commandments, or His Word, and in ancient times people were not able to see the tzitzit at night when it was dark. Traditionally the tallit is still not worn during an evening service with this one exception. Yet as believers in Yeshua, I believe we must be led by the Word of God and the Spirit of God and not place rabbinic law or Jewish tradition above either. Therefore, I encourage my congregation to wear the tallit as they are led of the Ruach HaKodesh. We don them during our evening services and have seen God move mightily as we sought Him in prayer under the tallit.

THE ORIGINS OF THE TALLIT

The wearing of the tallit commences in the Torah. We read in the fifteenth chapter of the Book of *Bamidbar* (Numbers):

> ADONAI spoke to Moses saying, "Speak to *Bnei-Yisrael* [children of Israel]. Say to them that they are to make for themselves *tzitzit* [fringes, ציצית] on the corners of their garments throughout their generations, and they are to put a blue cord on each *tzitzit*. It will be your own *tzitzit*—so whenever you look at them, you will remember all the *mitzvot* [commandments] of ADONAI and do them and not go spying out after your own hearts and your own eyes, prostituting yourselves. This way you will remember and obey all My *mitzvot* and you will be holy to your God. I am ADONAI your God. I brought you out of the land of Egypt to be your God. I am ADONAI your God."
>
> —NUMBERS 15:37–41

In ancient times people in most cultures wore some type of blanketlike garment to protect them from the sun during the day and the cool air at night. So the command in Numbers 15 was not for the Jewish people to start wearing this type of garment but rather for them to add the tzitzit on the four corners, which would set them apart from other nations. Even today Bedouins wear abayas, which can resemble the tallit but lack the tzitzit.

But God's purpose for having His people add tzitzit to their garments was not merely to set them apart from other peoples. As the Torah states, it was so they would be constantly reminded of God's commandments. God had entered into a covenant with His people and promised to bless them if they were faithful to His Word. The consequences for disobedience were severe, even death in some cases. (See Deuteronomy 28.) God's desire was that by wearing the tallit with the tzitzit, the Jewish people would be constantly reminded of His Word. And as they walked in obedience to His commands, they would experience His continued blessing in their lives. This is still Hashem's desire for us—that we would experience His blessing as we obey His Word and His voice.

Initially after the law regarding the tallit commenced, the tallit was worn much like a daily cloak and not only during times of prayer. But over time it became more of a religious garment, and by New Testament times the tallit was worn primarily on special occasions. The Pharisees, however, seemed to wear the tallit all the time, but it was often just for show. They wore extra-long fringes to prove their piety, a practice Yeshua condemned.

> "When you pray, do not be like the hypocrites; for
> they love to pray standing in the synagogues and
> on the street corners, so that they may be seen by

others. Amen, I tell you, they have their reward in full! But you, when you pray, go into your inner room; and when you have shut your door, pray to your Father who is in secret. And your Father, who sees in secret, shall reward you."

—MATTHEW 6:5–6

Hashem would never have us wear the tallit to appear righteous or holy. The tallit should always be worn in humility to bring honor to Hashem and to remember His Word to us, His children.

PARTS OF THE TALLIT

In this book we will discover the spiritual symbolism hidden within the tallit. But I first want to explain the significance of each part of the prayer shawl.

TZITZIT

As we have seen, the purpose of the tallit was to hold the tzitziyot, or fringes, to remind the people of the commands of God. The tzitziyot were to be tied on each of the garment's four corners so that when we look at the tallit, specifically the tzitzit, we would remember the commandments of God. Today there are T-shirts onto which the tzitzit may be tied at each of the four corners, illustrating again that the tzitzit are most important.

TEKHELET

Traditionally on each tzitzit is a blue cord called the *tekhelet*. According to some, the blue tekhelet is to remind us of God's creation, the ocean, the sky, the tablets upon which the Ten Commandments were written, and His throne of glory. It can also remind us that God's Word is from above and that His people are meant to reflect His heavenly kingdom on this earth.

The particular color blue used in the tekhelet was once very hard to acquire and was thus used on special garments. During antiquity it was derived from a type of snail found near the Aegean Sea, and it took thousands of snails to extract just a small amount of the dye. It has been thought that, after the destruction of the second temple, knowledge of the actual source of the dye was lost. For this reason, it is now common for the tzitzit to have only white fringes. It is believed that some of the species that carry the dye have been found, but that is not universally accepted as fact.

There are places in Israel today where you can purchase the tzitzit with the tekhelet. They can be tied on to the four corners of a garment to make a tallit. During one of the tours of Israel that my wife, Racquel, and I co-led with two other rabbis over twenty years ago, we met an Israeli storeowner who sold the tzitzit with the tekhelet. I purchased a tallit gadol and a tallit katan from him, and I still wear them today. There are also many websites that sell tallitot, some of which include the tekhelet.*

ATARAH

The tallit has an embroidered neckband called the *atarah*. The primary purpose of the atarah is to help the wearer distinguish the inside from the outside of the tallit

---

* To learn more about how to purchase a tallit, you can visit our website at www.gesherinternational.com.

and ensure the garment is not worn upside down. The atarah also contains the blessing that is recited when a person puts the tallit on his shoulders.

FORMING THE TZITZIT

Tying the tzitzit is something of an art, similar to macramé. According to the halacha, which is the rabbinical way, or "the body of Jewish law supplementing the scriptural law and forming the legal part of the Talmud,"[1] the tzitzit is made by tying a knot in a braid-like fashion using four threads that are interwoven into the four corners of a garment possessing four or more angular corners. The halacha has determined that the threads of the tzitzit must be passed through a hole at each end of the cloth and then multiplied by two to produce eight threads (one of which is longer than the others and is referred to as the *shamash*). The threads should then be tied in a well-fastened double knot.[2]

The shamash is then wound around the other threads, and additional knots are tied. There are various customs regarding winding and tying knots, but the two most common are of four groups of seven, eight, eleven, and thirteen *or* five, six, five, and ten windings with knots tied between them and at their end. Overall, there are five knots in the tzitzit.[3]

It is thought that the winding of the five, six, five, and ten represents the fifth, sixth, fifth, and tenth letters of the Hebrew alphabet. That would be yod, hey, vav, hey, as we read them from right to left: יהוה. Together these letters mean "Adonai" or "Lord." So the tzitzit represents

Hashem. Some also say the free-flowing fringes represent the Israelites' emancipation from Egypt.

DONNING THE TALLIT

To don the tallit, many will first unfold it and hold it in both hands so the atarah is facing them. Then they recite the blessing:

> *Baruch Atah Adonai, Eloheinu, melech ha'olam asher kidishanu b'mitz'votav v'tzivanu l'hit'ateif ba-tzitzit.* (Blessed are You, Lord, our God, King of the universe, who has sanctified us by His commandments and commanded us to wrap ourselves in the tzitzit.)

After reciting the blessing, the person will throw the tallit over his shoulders like a cape and then position it on his shoulders. Before positioning the tallit on their shoulders, some will bring their hands together in front of their face briefly and cover their head with the tallit for a moment of private meditation. Then they adjust the tallit comfortably on their shoulders. I believe it is good to know the proper way to don the tallit, but I always encourage people to keep their focus on God and not the ritual. Focusing on the ritual can keep us from entering into God's presence.

The tallit is generally draped or wrapped around the shoulders until it is time for prayer. At that time the wearer will cover his head with the tallit. Covering one's head with the tallit is symbolic of calling out to God and telling

Him we desire a time of intimacy with Him. The tallit is worn during most Jewish prayer services, and some keep their heads covered with the tallit during the entire liturgical portion of worship. It is customary for many men and women to also don their tallitot for individual prayer in their own personal prayer closets.

In our congregation we also use the tallit during a time when we pray for the children. We set three or four tallitot up as a very large chuppah (canopy) and have the children stand under it as we pray the Aaronic Benediction over them. Others in the congregation who need a special touch from Yeshua can also come stand under the tallit and receive this unique blessing from Numbers 6:24–26, which says: "The LORD bless you and keep you; the LORD make His face to shine upon you, and be gracious unto you; the LORD lift His countenance upon you, and give you peace" (MEV).

Some say Christians should not wear the prayer shawl because the laws regarding the tallit were given to the Jewish people under the Torah. While it is true that believers in Yeshua are not obligated to wear the tallit, because Yeshua became a bridge that joined those born Jewish and those not born Jewish together in Him as one new man, anyone who chooses to obey the Word of God can wear the tallit. As a result, many believers in Yeshua who were not born Jewish have experienced very special times of prayer under the tallit.

A SACRED GARMENT

So much detail goes into how a tallit is made and worn because it is considered a holy object. It represents Yeshua, His Word, and His covering and should always be worn with honor, love, and respect toward Hashem.

One Shabbat morning as I was preparing to enter the sanctuary and begin my services, I looked out the window and noticed a man drive up to the synagogue, find a parking spot, and proceed into the building. He cordially introduced himself to me as Rabbi So-and-So, and I told him how nice it was to meet him. But then I asked him, "Are you really a rabbi?" He seemed a bit taken aback and asked me why I would ask him that. I responded by telling him that most rabbis would know that you don't drive, especially on Shabbat, with your tallit as outer clothing and then allow your tzitzit to fall on the pavement as you walk to the synagogue.

As it turned out, the man was neither Jewish nor a rabbi, but he was interested in learning more about the garment that was worn by the Jewish Teacher, Yeshua. I told him we could make plans to meet at another time and I would be glad to teach him about the tallit.

On another occasion I went to a meeting on a weekday night where there was a special guest speaker and a tremendous amount of praise and worship music. People were rejoicing and feeling free to worship in various ways. Some of the behavior appeared strange to me, but I am open to whatever Hashem desires to do through His Ruach (Spirit). One man in the middle of the large hall was wearing a large tallit. Unfortunately, more of the tallit was on the floor than on his back. It really bothered me, but I decided to mind my own business.

As the service went on, I noticed that people were trampling over his tallit as they rushed to the front of the sanctuary for special prayer ministry. After seeing the tallit become like an area rug that was repeatedly being walked on, I decided to go over and say something to the young man, but he was lost in the crowd. I am sure that gentleman meant no harm, but holy objects should be worn with respect for the Holy One of Israel.

During weekly Saturday Shabbat services we have a Torah march. All who are able stand as the Torah is walked around the sanctuary. Although the congregation in a Messianic synagogue is made up of people born Jewish and not born Jewish (we are all one in Messiah), at this point in the service most of the men and a few of the women typically wear tallitot. When the Torah passes by, each person in the congregation who is wearing a tallit will touch the Torah with the tzitzit and then lift the tzitzit to his or her mouth and kiss it.

Some people who visit our congregation don't want to stand up and participate, even though we provide tallitot for those who need them (including feminine ones for the women). They believe we are practicing a worthless ritual that puts us in bondage. They are so wrong! The tzitzit represent the commandments, or the Word of God, and Yeshua is the Living Word (John 1:14). So spiritually, when we touch the tzitzit to our lips, we are giving the Teacher a kiss and receiving one from Him, as the Scripture says: "Let him kiss me with the kisses of his mouth! For your love is better than wine" (Songs 1:2, MEV). Kissing the tzitzit is symbolic of the Ruach's love touching us and bonding with our spirit. That is what takes place not only when we kiss the tzitzit during a service but also when the tallit is wrapped around us.

A SOURCE OF PROTECTION

The tallit reminds us of God's Word, and Hashem gave us His Word to guard us from pursuing the cravings of our flesh. He did this because He loves us. He knows our fleshly desire to return to our sin nature can cause us to stray from our close relationship with Yeshua.

I once knew a man who was in leadership and would always wear his tallit katan with his tzitzit showing. One day I noticed that he was not wearing it. When I asked him why, he said he just didn't want to wear it anymore. I thought his response was strange, but I accepted his answer. A few weeks later I found out that he had been caught having an affair. It was sad, but I realized that it is hard to be enticed into sin when wearing a tallit. Wearing the tallit katan would remind you of the holiness of God and not to give in to the cravings of your flesh. Giving in to these temporary pleasures is a form of idolatry because you are putting your temporary gratification ahead of your relationship with Hashem.

In addition to reminding us of God's holiness and protecting us from falling into sin, the tallit also serves as a literal protection for certain holy objects. In Judaism the Torah is considered the holiest book as the foundation of all the Scriptures, so the tallit is used to protect the scrolls of the Torah when they are moved. The tallit also protects other holy objects when they are worn out or unusable. An old, unusable tallit is donated to the synagogue or a Judaic library. It is then used to wrap worn-out or superfluous documents such as photocopies that include the name YHVH (יהוה) or Adonai (אדני), the sacred name of God in Hebrew script, which are buried with dignity in a *genizah*, a section of a Jewish cemetery set aside for this purpose.

The Teacher said, "You are the salt of the earth; but if the salt should lose its flavor, how shall it be made salty again? It is no longer good for anything, except to be thrown out and trampled under foot by men" (Matt. 5:13). Likewise, the holy object that loses its holiness would be rendered useless. The old holy objects that contain the name of God or that were used for holy events but are now torn or worn out should be treated with respect. Consequently the tallit must be wrapped around the holy object and buried with it, with one of the tzitzit cut off to make it invalid to be used for prayer. This practice of cutting off one of the corners of the tallit is also carried out when a tallit is buried with a person.

THE TALLIT IN LIFE-CYCLE EVENTS

To a Jewish person the tallit is symbolic of his Jewish identity because it is used in all the major life events—from birth to burial. Yeshua the Teacher is with us from the beginning of our lives—from the moment of conception—until the last day of our lives and unto eternity for those who choose to receive Him. The use of the tallit in each of these life events reflects God's presence with us throughout our lives. It is a reminder that He is with us and will never leave or forsake us (Deut. 31:6). If we don't experience Him, it is because we are not looking for His love notes!

THE TALLIT IN BIRTH

Eight days after a male child is born, he is circumcised. During the *bris* (also called a *brit milah*), or circumcision, the father wraps the dressed infant in his tallit for a few moments and prays over the baby. In doing this, the father is symbolically wrapping the baby in the Word of God and the covering of Hashem. During this ceremony the father, the *sandek* (or godfather, who has the role of holding the child on his lap during the blessings, as he and the godmother are supposed to look out for and guide their godchildren into maturity), and the *mohel* (the one who performs the circumcision) all wear tallitot. Consequently, the wearing of the tallit is again a reminder of the magnificent presence of the Most High God! For girls there is a naming dedication ceremony that takes place eighty days after they are born.

THE TALLIT IN BAR/BAT MITZVAH

The tallit is again used at a child's bar or bat mitzvah. This is a time when the young person is thought to come of age. He or she is presented with a tallit, and during the ceremony the young man or woman reads from the Torah, haftarah, and possibly the B'rit Chadashah if the family has embraced Yeshua as Messiah. The theme for this public reading is the same throughout each portion.

The new adult is now taking on the responsibility of following the Word of God by becoming a son or daughter of the commandments. The child is responsible for his or her words and actions in the community. This person is now able to wear his or her new tallit to synagogue and other events that require it. Once again, everything is done to acknowledge the presence of Yeshua in our lives.

THE TALLIT IN MARRIAGE

The tallit is again used in marriage. The tallit is placed on poles and is used to create a canopy called a chuppah. The man and woman then come together under the chuppah of God. Marriage is an institution that was created by Hashem before sin took place in the Garden of Eden (*Gan Eden*). "ADONAI *Elohim* caused a deep sleep to fall on the man and he slept; and He took one of his ribs and closed up the flesh in its place. ADONAI *Elohim* built the rib, which He had taken from the man, into a woman. Then He brought her to the man. Then the man said, 'This one, at last, is bone of my bones and flesh from my flesh. This one is called woman, for from man was taken this one.' This is why a man leaves his father and his mother and clings to his wife; and they become one flesh [*basar echad*]" (Gen. 2:21–24). As Yeshua said, "What God has joined together, let no man separate!" (Mark 10:9).

Marriage represents the completion of the image of God. It represents the oneness, the *basar echad*, the unique composite that results from the coming together of man and woman. Consequently, our marriage reflects our walk with the Messiah. Under the tallit a man and woman bond together in marriage. It is no longer about him or her; it is about them as a couple. In marriage selfishness is no longer an option. We must love our spouse as Yeshua loves us. The Teacher tells us to "do nothing out of selfishness or conceit, but with humility consider others as more important than yourselves" (Phil. 2:3).

As a couple stands under the tallit in the marriage ceremony, they are joined together with Hashem as a three-stranded cord. His presence is in the midst of them. Marriage begins a new creation as instituted by our Creator. The couple entered the space under the tallit as individuals and leave it with a new "oneness" that is reflected in the unity of God. As His powerful will stands in the center of this new creation, the couple realizes that it is His will that must lead and guide them throughout their lives.

THE TALLIT IN DEATH AND BURIAL

The tallit, as with the other life-cycle events, is used in death. Those who have a tallit that has been passed down from generation to generation or who have a special tallit might desire to be buried in it. The tallit does not signify death. It epitomizes life in God's presence and the covering of His powerful Word. It embodies Yeshua's message of repentance, resurrection, and eternal life. Death is not the end. It is the beginning of an unimaginable eternity for those who know the Messiah.

When a tallit is used in burial, we must remember that it is a sign of holiness and sanctification. In life the individual wearing the tallit should be one who is set apart as unto Hashem. It should be worn by one who wants to be a light unto the nations. People should be able to look at this person and see something different about him or her and want that same special quality. The difference they see is the Spirit of Adonai.

A person should be buried in a tallit only if it represents who the individual was in life. Was the individual a man or woman of faith? Did he or she follow the commandments of Yeshua? Was the person one who tried to love his neighbor as himself? The Teacher followed all the commandments perfectly. Did the deceased person model his or her life after Yeshua? Was the person prideful or humble? Was the person judgmental? Was the person generous or greedy? Was he or she a person of prayer? Was the individual a person of character and integrity? These questions must be considered when determining whether to bury someone in a tallit because it represents a love and respect for Hashem.

We know that the tallit, the garment to hold the tzitzit, was first spoken of in the Torah. Nevertheless, as we progress in our reading of the Tanakh and B'rit Chadashah (Old and New Testaments), Yeshua reveals to us more spiritual meanings of the tallit. It is more than a physical garment. Everything Yeshua gives us has a physical and a spiritual purpose. There is so much more to receive. Let's continue our journey to understand the tallit as we learn about hearing God under the tallit.

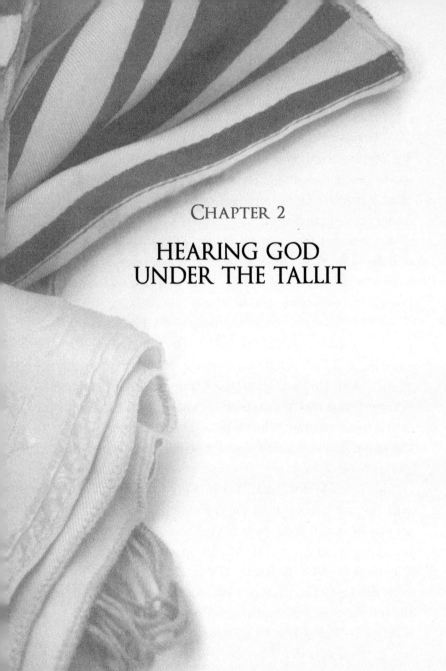

CHAPTER 2

HEARING GOD
UNDER THE TALLIT

THE TERM *TALLIT* is often said to mean "little tent" because the Hebrew word *tal* can be translated "tent." However, the word *tallit* actually means "to cover." The Hebrew word *tal* is literally translated "dew," and just as the dew covers the grass in the morning, so does the tallit symbolize God's presence covering us as we come under the tallit in prayer.

Yet it is not incorrect to define *tallit* as a "little tent," and doing so creates a fitting picture. When worn over the head, the tallit becomes a "little tent," allowing us to shut out distractions as we seek Hashem in prayer.

In Old Testament times the people of Israel were too numerous for everyone to fit into the tent of meeting. In the tallit each man had his own private sanctuary in which to meet with God and give Him his undivided attention. Perhaps this is why Yeshua tells us in Matthew 6:6 to enter into a closet to pray. When a person covers himself with the prayer shawl, he shuts out the world. It becomes his "prayer closet."

The Torah tells us that, "When all the people saw the pillar of cloud standing at the entrance of the Tent, they all rose up and worshipped, every man at the entrance of his own tent. So ADONAI spoke with Moses face to face, as a man speaks with his friend" (Exod. 33:10–11).

When I read this passage, I imagine the "pillar of cloud," the holy presence of Hashem, falling upon the *K'lal Yisrael* (the "whole of Israel") and then as Moses proceeds to go out to speak with El Shaddai, the people exit their tents and stand under their own tallit and wait patiently for Hashem to speak to them. Today we can symbolically do the same thing as we temporarily exit our secular realm and enter into the spiritual realm under our own tallit, being secluded with Him for the purpose of just worshipping and listening to His word for us.

Why do we need to shut ourselves off in prayer? This is how we can get alone with Yeshua and hear clearly from Him. Have you ever been focused in prayer only to suddenly have a random thought come to mind? It might be a reminder to return someone's call or respond to an e-mail. Having the tallit over our heads helps keep us focused in our personal prayer space so we can discern the voice of Hashem and block out the background noise.

We see an example of this in 1 Kings:

> After the fire there was a soft whisper of a voice. As soon as Elijah heard it, he wrapped his face in his mantle [tallit], went out and stood at the entrance of the cave. Then all of a sudden, a voice addressed him and said, "What are you doing here Elijah?"
>
> —1 Kings 19:12–13

When Elijah wrapped himself in the tallit, he was able to focus and concentrate. Then he could hear the voice of Adonai. How do we hear God? We meditate under the tallit and block out all distractions.

When we position the tallit over our heads and close our eyes in worship, we can experience intimacy with God. He longs to come near and allow us to experience His presence. He is there, under the tallit or wherever "there" is, just waiting for us to seek Him. He wants to communicate with us, but are we willing to listen?

BACK TO THE GARDEN

Communication between man and God began in the Garden of Eden: "Then *ADONAI Elohim* formed the man out of the dust from the ground and He breathed into his nostrils a breath of life—so the man became a living being. Then *ADONAI Elohim* planted a garden in Eden in the east, and there He put the man whom He had formed" (Gen. 2:7–8).

Rabbinic commentators believe Adam was formed outside the garden in a land of thorns and thistles, where he would eat food by the sweat of his brow. They believe this is why we read that "*ADONAI Elohim* took the man and gave him rest in the Garden of Eden in order to cultivate and watch over it" (Gen. 2:15). When Adam was placed in the Gan Eden, which is paradise, there was a continual, everlasting *kesher* (connection) and communication with God. This everlasting kesher is the fullness of prayer and meditation.

Before sin entered the world, Adam enjoyed total peace and rest as he watched over and cultivated the garden because he was in the presence of Adonai. This is the goal of prayer and meditation. Outside the garden Adam had to work by the sweat of his brow against thorns and thistles because he was not in Hashem's presence. Being inside or outside the garden represents the two paths humankind would have to choose between. On one path man gives in to temptation, desiring to make himself higher than Hashem. On the other path man chooses to avoid sin and remain in paradise for eternity.

As the story of mankind continued, it became obvious

that no person could ever be without sin, and therefore no one could live in the Gan Eden. However, Yeshua, who was both man and God, was sinless. Only through Him would the flaming swords of the cherubim be removed so man could enter the garden and live with Hashem for eternity. When we pray, it is by His *chesed* (lovingkindness or grace) and our faith or trust that we are delivered from the thorns and thistles of sin to the Shabbat of everlasting shalom!

This is the fullness of prayer. When we interact and find that special connection with Yeshua, we are taken on a journey in our everyday life from the "thorns and thistles" of life into the paradise of His presence. On which path do you choose to travel?

DEEP CALLS TO DEEP UNDER THE TALLIT

Meditation—being still in the presence of Yeshua and listening for His voice—should be the foremost function of our prayer life. Scripture says, "Deep calls to deep in the roar of Your waterfalls" (Ps. 42:8). Years ago when I was at the State University of New York at Buffalo, I used to travel every so often to visit Niagara Falls. You could hear the roar from the flow of the millions of gallons of water that soar over the top and plunge to its depth at the bottom. It was magnificent! When I think of deep calling to deep, I think of this image—of entering deeper and deeper into the multitude of dimensions of the spirit as we take the plunge into His presence.

When I was in college, many people thought that only

through the use of certain substances and trips to gurus in the East could we enter into the deep meditation of the soul to find truth. When I chanted words and syllables of Eastern religions that probably have their origin in ancient Babylon, they just fell flat, as if I were speaking to a stone or a piece of wood. But through prayer and meditation with Yeshua we can find the truth.

As we enter into His presence through prayer, we need to be still and receive from Him. He wants to fill us with His joy and goodness. As we seek Him under the tallit, we must ruminate upon His Word and receive His instructions for us each day. When we speak repeatedly to His Spirit, read devotionals, and ponder His direction for us in peace and quiet, there is a renewal of life and hope. Fear and doubt flee away, and His words become life and reality. When we take the plunge into His Spirit, sensing the limitless depth of His being, we might feel like we are entering into the third heaven, as Rabbi Shaul (Paul the Apostle) described in 2 Corinthians 12:2. As we cleave to His existence through prayer and meditation, we become strong, resolute, and ready to do battle as a soldier in His militia.

I learned to say the Shema at the age of five because it was (and still is) the foundational prayer of our faith. I would speak to God and ask Him to bless my loved ones. That prayer connected me with my Jewish people throughout the world and throughout history. I love the words and meaning of this prayer, and I begin my quiet time with Yeshua almost always with the Shema ("Hear, O Israel, the LORD is our God, the LORD is One"). There have been many times when I came to synagogue on Shabbat feeling anxious or discouraged or worried about something, but when the liturgy began, I began to experience His presence. The distractions in my mind departed and I was filled with joy.

However, praying the Shema is not meditation. Meditation takes me into the depth of God's Spirit. Meditating in the presence of Yeshua builds trust and brings an exceptionally high state of serenity, an ecstasy of devotion, and an excitement of love. "You keep in perfect peace one whose mind is stayed on You, because he trusts in You. Trust in ADONAI forever, for the LORD ADONAI is a Rock of ages" (Isa. 26:3–4). Meditation is "deep calling unto deep"!

The more time we spend in Hashem's presence, the better we will come to know His voice. The Spirit of God speaks often to us and through us, but most times people are so busy and bogged down with mundane things that they don't hear His voice. When Racquel and I were seeking to "find God," He was there all the time. We just didn't know how to recognize His voice. However, as we walked more and more with Yeshua, we learned how to discern what He was saying. How did we know it was Yeshua speaking? We learned that if what we heard did not line up with the Word, then it was not the Teacher's voice we were hearing. When we originally heard Him speak to our hearts and minds at the same time during our visit to a church (for more on this experience see the appendix), His words lined up with the Torah, which says He will send to us a prophet like Moses. (See Deuteronomy 18:15, 18.) As a result our lives were turned upside down.

"Faith comes from hearing, and hearing by the word of

Messiah" (Rom. 10:17). The Teacher is the Word of God! He is that "Unique One," the living Word who "became flesh and dwelt among us" (John 1:14, MEV). So as we get to know Him, we get to know His voice. We get to know the voice of our God as sheep get to know the voice of their shepherd (John 10:27).

In 1990 I heard the voice of Hashem speak to my heart and tell me to read *The Hiding Place* by Corrie ten Boom. I couldn't imagine why, but I was obedient. At that time Racquel and I were looking to move from Plantation, Florida, to Boca Raton. We wanted to rent for a year because we were planning on moving up to Palm Beach Gardens. After searching for a long time and seeing many properties, we just couldn't find the place we knew Yeshua had for us. When you come to know the Teacher, you discern His path for you. Of course, you can misinterpret what He is saying. However, He will always lead you back in the correct direction.

We began to wonder if we had made an error. We called out to Yeshua and asked Him to guide us. We prayed intensely. All of a sudden, one day while we were looking for properties and riding through the neighborhoods in west Boca Raton, we saw a development we hadn't seen previously. It was called Escondido, which means "hidden" or "the hiding place." Yes, I did hear from Hashem! I read the great book by Corrie ten Boom, but Yeshua was also telling me without my understanding that He was sending us to a certain house in a certain location in Boca Raton. The best part was that the house was beautiful and had everything we desired!

We need to make sure the words of Yeshua are upon

our hearts, souls, minds, and spirits. The Teacher abides in our hearts, so we must pay attention to what He is saying, especially in this most intimate setting as we are covered in the tallit. As we wait in His presence under the tallit, our love for Him will increase and our spiritual hearing will become sharper. There are different instances when we need advice for ourselves or to give to someone. We don't want to speak words that have no lasting effect. However, in a moment Yeshua could give you a word from His throne room that could change the outcome of your life or the lives of others who are looking for advice.

When Miriam (Mary) heard all the things that were prophesied about the One to whom she was giving birth, she pondered them in her heart. (See Luke 2:15–19.) She had heard the divine truth that was spoken to her spirit, and she believed. When "deep calls to deep," we must listen, act, and allow the words we hear to sink into our spirit man.

HEARING AND OBEYING THE WORD

I recently had a conversation with a successful businessman. He asked me about my dreams and thoughts for the next stage of my life. As I told him my plans, he asked me, "Why don't you just do it now?" I began to explain to him that I had to know if the Spirit of God was instructing me and to wait for His timing to make any changes. This sounded like foolishness to him. He said one reason for his success is that he gets an idea and then just does what he wants to do. He said he is the one in charge of his life.

I proceeded to explain to him that my life is totally submitted to the *Ruach Elohim* (Spirit of God). I have submitted myself to being led by His Spirit for the last thirty years, and I can't make a major life change until I know the instructions come from Him. How do we know when the Spirit of God is leading? He speaks to our mind and heart at the same time, and we just know that it is Hashem speaking.

He who belongs to God hears the words of God. The reason we don't hear is because either we have not learned to discern His voice or there is so much background noise that we can't recognize which voice is His! To some reading this book, being led by the voice of God may sounds like foolishness. But Hashem said through one of His prophets, "The wisdom of their wise will perish, and the discernment of their discerning will be concealed" (Isa. 29:14).

My successful friend, whom I admire, could not grasp what I was saying. He didn't understand that when you discern the Spirit's voice, you must also wait on His perfect timing. Our society urges us to be assertive and follow our urges and fulfill our desires. Yet waiting under the tallit to hear God's voice brings triumph and joy to our lives. Trials and tribulations do come, but He promises to be with us wherever we go.

How do we know when and if it is His timing? How do we know that we didn't make a mistake and waste years of our lives? When Hashem is speaking to us, it can be verified by His Word, by wisdom from elders, and/or by signs and circumstances. We can see the fruit of our journey and know if it was indeed Adonai who called us. In the spirit realm we must wait on God to hear His voice.

We are always tempted to act before we hear. To follow this temptation is impatience, and impatience is a type of pride. It is taking the matter into our own hands because we think Hashem is taking too long. It is the act of not being totally dependent upon Him. It is the opposite of humility.

Over and over Yeshua has instructed us to wait for Him. This submission to Him is a test of our faith. We do not seek to lift ourselves up but to bring honor to His holy name. This life is not about us but all about Him and advancing His kingdom!

When the great prophet Samuel was just a boy who had been dedicated to Adonai's service under Eli the *kohen* (priest) by his mother, Hannah, he heard a voice saying, "Samuel! Samuel!" After hearing the voice of Adonai for a third time, Samuel responded, "Speak, for Your servant is listening" (1 Sam. 3:10). Adonai spoke to Samuel, and Samuel relayed the message to Eli as God had instructed him. As Samuel grew up, he always listened and was obedient to Adonai, and all Israel knew that "Samuel was entrusted as a prophet of ADONAI" (1 Sam. 3:20). Eli, on the other hand, had heard the words of God but did not listen. As a result he and his sons received a rebuke and were cursed instead of being blessed by Hashem. (See 1 Samuel 3:11–14.)

The Spirit of God had spoken to my wife and me to pray for one of our daughters to conceive. We didn't know if our daughter and son-in-law had been trying to have a baby, but we obeyed and prayed every day for the child that would eventually be in her womb. After a few months the Spirit told us to pray now for the child in her womb.

Some weeks afterward our daughter and her husband told us that there was indeed a baby in her womb! Again, how awesome it is to hear the voice of Yeshua speak to you and see the amazing results of your obedience!

IN THE PRAYER CLOSET OF THE TALLIT

From the first man, Adam, to the time when the last person will be born, Yeshua has spoken and will continue to speak to us. He is looking to communicate with the person who has a sanctified heart, a heart that is set apart to be intimate with the One who is responsible for all creation! The Spirit of the living God spoke to Jeremiah the prophet and said, "Call to Me, and I will answer you—I will tell you great and hidden things, which you do not know" (Jer. 33:3).

The Teacher also spoke by His Spirit through Rabbi Shaul: "We do speak wisdom, however, among those who are mature—but not a wisdom of this age or of the rulers of this age, who are coming to nothing. Rather, we speak God's wisdom in a mystery—a wisdom that has been hidden, which God destined for our glory before the ages" (1 Cor. 2:6–7).

As I write this book, I have been suffering from plantar fasciitis for over four months. There is pain with every step I take. About three months ago I was on vacation and met a medical doctor who specialized in acupuncture, so I decided to try that method of treatment for the pain. He told me I would need more than one session. He said that initially the impurities must be removed so the things that are deep and hidden can come to the surface. Then with a subsequent treatment he could get rid of the poison causing the inflammation.

This is a perfect illustration of why we must listen to God under the tallit. There are many voices vying for our attention, but we find the truth when we eliminate the "background noise"—all the poisonous and inflammatory voices that lead us on the wrong path. We can only remove the noise when we spend our time in communication with Yeshua.

By the way, when this Buddhist doctor explained his treatment process to me, I shared with him the spiritual insight I gained from his words. To my wonderful surprise, he received my words with joy and excitement and asked me to pray for him to receive Yeshua, the Messiah, into his heart. Each time I saw him afterward, he was filled with thanksgiving!

The people of Israel heard the voice of Adonai at Mount Sinai, but they became so fearful that they asked Moses to be the intermediary between them and Adonai. When God spoke, there was thunder and lightning, the sound of the shofar, and smoke on the mountain. (See Exodus 19:16–19.) Everyone in the camp trembled and stood far off. They thought if God spoke with them directly, they would die. They had experienced the true and living God.

The God of glory thunders. He is over mighty waters. The voice of Adonai is powerful. The voice of Adonai is full of majesty. The voice of Adonai breaks the cedars and hews out flames of fire. The voice of Adonai shakes the desert. He sits as King forever. He gives strength to His people and blesses His people with shalom. (See

Psalm 29.) But this powerful God also desires to communicate with us.

We are to have reverent fear of Hashem. We must recognize His majesty and awe-inspiring presence and power. Yet because of His everlasting love for us, He has chosen to abide with mankind through the Ruach HaKodesh! And as we listen to and obey our Creator, our intimacy with Him grows.

God is trying to permeate our spiritual atmosphere with His goodness, blessings, signs, and miracles, but as Bible teacher and worship leader Tiffany Ann Lewis wrote, "at the same time His kingdom is under attack. The enemy is trying to steal our joy, our peace, our prosperity, our healing, and all of our blessings, as well as trying to keep us defeated and discouraged" so we do not believe that His miraculous power and the fire of His Spirit are for us or for our current situation.[1] But we cannot give up. We must press into God through prayer, for "the effective prayer of a righteous person is very powerful" (Jacob [James] 5:16).[2]

INTERCESSORY PRAYER

Just as Yeshua seeks to meet our needs in prayer, He is calling us to intercede for others in our prayer closet under the tallit. We see the power of intercession in the life of King David:

> Then David built there an altar to ADONAI, and offered burnt offerings and fellowship offerings. So

> ADONAI was moved by prayer of entreaty for the
> land, and restrained the plague from Israel.
> —2 SAMUEL 24:25

Intercessory prayer is a supplication, a plea in which
we implore Yeshua to act on someone else's behalf. It is a
true humbling or prostration of our souls.

Intercession is a way of loving others. In intercession the focus shifts from our own needs to the needs of
others. It is taking up the yoke of Messiah! We are vessels
of Hashem through which captives are being set free, the
blind are seeing, the deaf are hearing, the good news is
being brought to the afflicted, shattered marriages are
being healed, children who were being destroyed are being
restored, relationships are being reconciled, and the sick
are being healed. When we prayed and interceded continuously for our daughter to get pregnant, she did. The
Teacher is waiting to hear from us so He can bless us and
those around us.

One time my wife and I were on our way to a conference. We had just boarded the plane, and I believed
Yeshua was speaking to me through His Spirit. I prayed
for discernment and really believed that there was something wrong with the plane. Racquel and I prayed and
prayed that if there was a problem, He would stop the
flight. Everything continued as if there were no malfunction. The plane started to take off by speeding up, and I
prayed in a voice that only my wife could hear, "Oh Lord,
if there is anything wrong with the plane, *stop it now!*"

As I said, "Stop it now," the plane came to a screeching
halt. The pilot said there was some malfunction and

that we needed to go back and deplane so we could take another plane! Our prayers and the prayers of the many people interceding for our trip combined with the intercession of those praying for other passengers touched the heart of Yeshua, and we were all led to safety. He is in control of all things from eternity to eternity. Sometimes Hashem allows things to happen so we can humbly submit to Him and call upon His name.

Years ago Racquel and I were interceding for her father's health. He was dying and suffering with much pain. He grew up in Orthodox Judaism, but when he left his home, he decided not to go to synagogue because in the time he spent there in his youth, he felt he was being forced to worship in a way that was not pleasing to him.

Many people, unfortunately, grow up with anger toward their parents because they were forced to believe a certain way. However, I do believe that if you "train up a child in the way he should go, when he is old he will not turn from it" (Prov. 22:6). Because of my excellent religious education as a child and teen, and my parents' wonderful example of having a relationship with Hashem, when I came to know Yeshua, I wanted to walk just like Him and be an observant Jewish man, as He was during His time here on earth. When I used to speak to my father-in-law about Yeshua, he naturally rejected what I was saying. However, he saw a change in my wife and me after we began to follow Yeshua, so he let me show him where the Teacher is written about in the Torah. All of a sudden his spiritual eyes opened and he began to understand what I was saying about Yeshua.

Some years later, as my father-in-law was nearing the end of his life, we interceded for him because he was semicomatose. We prayed, "Lord, if it is Your will, wake him up from the sleep and let me speak to him about You so he can receive You in his heart." Miraculously he came out of his semicomatose condition and allowed me to tell him about Yeshua. I said, "If you really want Him to enter your heart and you really mean what you are saying, then say *amein*." (This is how *amen* is usually pronounced in Hebrew.) With his physical eyes wide open, he shouted a loud and definitive, "*Amein!*" He then proceeded to close his eyes and go back to sleep. A short time later he went to live eternally with the Teacher.

THE POWER OF FASTING

Fasting is a true humbling of oneself before Adonai. As we fast and see the blessings of Hashem, our faith and trust in God increases. Fasting is a powerful tool in spiritual warfare.

Nehemiah was distraught after hearing about Jerusalem and the condition of the remnant who had survived the captivity. "Upon hearing these words I sat down and wept and mourned for days. I prayed and fasted before the God of heaven" (Neh. 1:4). A short time after Nehemiah poured out his heart and soul to *Shaddai* (the Almighty), King Artaxerxes gave him favor and granted his request to travel to Jerusalem and rebuild the city.

Ezra was bringing the patriarchal leaders, their families, and their genealogical records from Babylon back to Jerusalem, where the second temple had been built. However, the enemies of Israel were surrounding them, so they needed protection. We read in the Book of Ezra:

> Then I proclaimed a fast there at the Ahava River so
> that we might humble ourselves before our God and
> seek from Him a straight way for us, our little ones,
> and all of our possessions. For I was ashamed to ask
> the king for soldiers and cavalry to protect us from
> the enemy along the way, because we had spoken to
> the king saying, "The gracious hand of our God is
> upon everyone who seeks Him, but His great anger
> is against everyone who forsakes Him." So we fasted
> and sought our God about this, and He responded
> to our plea.
> —EZRA 8:21–23

In the battles of life and the valleys of decision, we need the power of Yeshua. One wrong decision could change a person's whole life. Fasting gets us closer to Him and enables us to hear His voice in a more distinct way. In our congregation, we have designated every Tuesday as a day of fasting. When we get together and break our fast after our time of praying, we experience a powerful move of God's Ruach! How awesome it is that Yeshua gives us the weapons of warfare so we can get close to Him, be protected, and win the battle! The Teacher Himself began His ministry with a forty-day fast. How many of us begin a new ministry, job, relationship, or calling by bathing it in prayer and fasting until we see an actual move of Hashem? We have seen many children begin fasting at Yom Kippur. Those who have fasted have done so because they wanted to bless Hashem. So many of them have grown up and developed into beautiful young adults. It is not because of the ritual but because they have been brought up to honor the Almighty in all they do. Many people seem to fast regularly but make no change in their lives. When our hearts are right with God, He gives us the power to make changes that last. However, we must want to change. "Why have we fasted, yet You do not see? Why have we afflicted our souls, yet You take no notice?" (Isa. 58:3). Shaddai answered that our behavior had not changed. We were still seeking our own pleasure and still exploiting our laborers. We were fasting for strife and contention and to strike with a wicked fist (Isa. 58:3–4).

When we fast, Yeshua wants us to be more like Him. If we are calling upon His name and using Him as our example, then our words and deeds must show it. Are we totally surrendering ourselves to Him? Are we fasting by afflicting our souls so that we love our neighbors and ask Yeshua to show us how we can help them? Are we praying and fasting so that His Spirit can work in us to help release the bonds of wickedness, to let the oppressed go free, and to tear off every yoke?

Are we willing to release the yoke of finger-pointing and bad-mouthing? Can we release the anger, bitterness, and slander we have toward our friends or neighbors and desire to be new people in Yeshua? Do we share our bread with the hungry and help support the homeless and poor? Do we pray and fast with an expectancy for healing, redemption, reconciliation, and restoration? If we do, then our righteousness will go before us, and the glory of Adonai will answer (Isa. 58:8). These are the things that should take place in our deep prayer, fasting, and meditation.

Too many of us follow rituals by rote but do not really

afflict our souls so that we may be changed in order to work for the kingdom of God. The Teacher wants us to conduct our fasts so that we are seen by Him and not for the purpose of impressing men. When you think of physical war on our planet today, you know that, in order to win the battle, there must be strong leadership, a vision, a plan, brilliant strategy, and a house not divided. It is the same way in spiritual warfare. If we follow Yeshua's guidelines, we will have victory!

In our lives there are many times when we are battling our enemy. The enemy doesn't have to be a person; it could be areas of doubt, discouragement, frustration, anger, bitterness, lust, or pride. There are times when we need to fast so Yeshua will renew our minds.

My wife and I began a new congregation in Orlando, Florida, in 2004. Before we began the synagogue, we fasted for God's power and strength. On August 13, 2004, we had fasted and prayed, and had intercessors praying for us. We were ready to begin. Then Hurricane Charley came on the scene, forcing us to cancel our first synagogue service. The newspapers in Orlando declared, "Charley Takes Orlando by Storm." We weren't discouraged by the fact that we had to cancel the service because we believed that headline was a prophetic word for our ministry. We too would take Orlando by storm!

Esther called for a three-day fast, and as a result the Jewish people were saved from destruction. Hannah prayed and fasted when she wanted Adonai to give her a child, and she gave birth to Samuel, who became a prophet. King David fasted when he wanted to show his grief for Abner, son of Ner, who was killed. In Judaism we afflict our souls by going a full day without food or water for Yom Kippur, the Day of Atonement. This day is considered the holiest day in the Jewish calendar because we afflict our souls for the purpose of getting close to Adonai and receiving His forgiveness for our sins. Even when we are in an intimate relationship with Yeshua, the Day of Atonement is still a time for us to fast food and water and afflict our souls. Through the Messiah we have our sins forgiven, but we stand with our people and pray and fast for their redemption, as we have received ours.

It always helps to fast so that we can truly discern El Shaddai's direction. In our everyday lives, when we are faced with danger, grief, or a life-changing decision, by continuous prayer and fasting we will hear from Yeshua, and He will show us His divine will for that situation.

THERE IS POWER IN PRAYER ... EVEN TO MOVE BUS STOPS

When my wife and I lived in Boca Raton, we had a beautiful home in a neighborhood with many children. We moved there in the summer, and it was peaceful and quiet. However, when school began in August, all of a sudden my wife and I were awakened every morning around 6:30 by the sounds of children yelling and screaming as they waited for the school bus right near our house. There was one young boy whose voice was especially loud; it was piercing and jarring. All we could do was pray and ask Yeshua to help us.

A couple of weeks passed, and the situation was the same. Suddenly, one morning we realized that we hadn't been awakened and it was not a school holiday. When I inquired as to what might have caused the children, especially that particular little boy, to be quiet, to my amazement and elation I discovered that the bus stop had been moved to another street! How awesome is that? The power of prayer can move mountains and bus stops!

Spending quality time with Yeshua sets us free to be the people Hashem desires us to be. As the lover of our souls, our *yedid nefesh* or "beloved," He draws us near to Him. When we focus our minds on Him and seek His face with hearts of true gratitude, the Teacher gives us the power and fire of His Spirit. A strong prayer life that includes meditating on His Word and His goodness can enable us to break through spiritual chains. There is nothing impossible with Him. Is His power limited? Is Adonai's arm too short? Absolutely not!

BE STILL
UNDER THE TALLIT

When we come under the tallit in prayer, we are to be still and know that He is God. We are to hide in His presence. We are to find that hidden place where we can commune with God. He is *HaMakom*—"the place"! Joshua commanded the *kohanim*, or priests, who were carrying the ark of the covenant to "stand still in the Jordan" when they reached the water's edge (Josh. 3:8). Why stand still? Because then the miracles would come!

> It will come to pass when the soles of the feet of the *kohanim* who are carrying the ark of ADONAI,

Sovereign of all the earth, *rest in the waters of the Jordan* [emphasis added], the Jordan's waters will be cut off. The waters coming downstream will stand up in one heap.

—JOSHUA 3:13

As they were going down toward the edge of town, Samuel said to Saul, "Tell your servant to go ahead of us and pass on, but as for you, *stand still awhile*, so that I may proclaim to you the word of God."

—1 SAMUEL 9:27,
EMPHASIS ADDED

Every day we face problems and situations that we need the wisdom of Hashem to handle. Many times we are so panicked and fearful that we just can't think straight. If we stand still under the tallit and come into His presence, we will find peace and be able to hear the *Kol Hashem* (voice of God).

A time is coming when there will be a famine for the Word of God. "'Behold, days are coming'—declares my Lord ADONAI—'when I will send a famine on the land—not a famine of bread, nor a thirst for water, but of hearing the words of ADONAI. So people will wander from sea to sea and roam from north to east, searching for the word of ADONAI, but they will not find it'" (Amos 8:11–12). This is why we must be still and know God now! As Yeshua said, "It is written, 'Man shall not live by bread alone, but by every word that comes from the mouth of God'" (Matt. 4:4).

When we hear the Teacher's voice, we accelerate forward in our search for spiritual intimacy with the Creator.

However, this doesn't mean that we will have a smooth and velvety, unbroken path. Usually it means just the opposite: the path will be rough and rocky. On this spiritual search we must be able to discern His voice and tune out all of the alien ones. It is those foreign voices that lead us off the right path by causing our spiritual hearing to become sluggish. How do we know which voice is His? The Spirit of Hashem lives within us and teaches us all things.

When we are still and spend time alone with Him, then we will know that He is God. He will reveal many hidden things to us as we wait, listen, and meditate in His presence under the tallit. Hashem will reveal to us the mysteries of the prayer shawl and other hidden treasures. We will know the truth, and the truth will set us free. The voice of the Teacher brings a peace beyond our understanding. It flows through us, tranquil and without ripples. Hearkening to His words and meditating upon them will cause us to begin to know the Shepherd!

When Yeshua comes to the place of highest importance in our lives, we can walk with great confidence in Him. A powerful prayer life can reframe the way we think and how we tackle difficult situations. The Teacher wants us to make right decisions and live in His presence and the fire of His Spirit. How blessed we are to be invited daily to come under the tallit of Hashem!

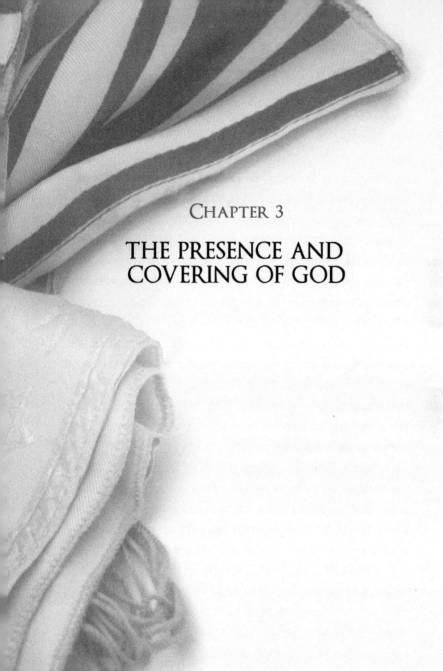

THE PRESENCE AND COVERING OF GOD

A FEW MONTHS AGO, a couple asked me to officiate their wedding. Though the ceremony was to be informal, they desired the presence of Hashem. I agreed to perform the ceremony and offered to host their wedding in my home. They were excited and asked if they could be married under a chuppah, which is a canopy the bride and groom stand under in Jewish weddings.

The chuppah symbolizes the covering and presence of God in a couple's life and marriage. A yarmulke, or *kippah,* also represents the covering of God, but standing under the tallit in the chuppah shows God's presence being wrapped around the bridegroom and the bride and the marriage covenant itself. This couple absolutely desired the covering of God upon them, so when I told them we could use a tallit to create a chuppah to cover their heads, they were ecstatic. When their big day came, the anointing and presence of Yeshua was powerful as this couple stood under the tallit.

I have performed many marriage ceremonies on the beach, and we have experienced the same powerful presence of Yeshua there as the waves crashed at our feet. Why? It was because several men held up the tallit so the couple would be married under a chuppah.

I officiated a wedding recently that was held outside under a large gazebo. Was that symbolic of the covering of God? No. However, the tallit, which was right above where the couple stood under the gazebo, did represent His covering, and the presence of Yeshua was awesome! The couple became an *echad,* a composite "one," just as God is an *echad,* a composite "one." Remember, it is not the garment itself that makes the tallit special but the tzitzit that are attached to the four corners, which represent the Word of God. When you are wrapped up or covered by His Word, you always experience the presence of *El Shaddai*, Almighty God.

As was evident at these wedding ceremonies, the tallit is a symbol of the covering and presence of God because His covering is His presence. This is yet another treasure that can be found when you experience the mystery of the prayer shawl. Just as the tallit covers the bride and groom when it serves as a chuppah during marriage ceremonies, so does the tallit symbolize Hashem's covering and presence when we come under it in prayer. When we cover ourselves in the tallit, we are symbolically inviting the Ruach HaKodesh to be present in our lives, and we are surrendering to His spiritual authority. In this chapter we will be discussing various aspects of His presence, covering, and delegated authority as He extends His tallit over our lives.

COMING INTO THE PRESENCE OF HASHEM

King David was a worshipper and a prayer warrior. The Psalms attest to this. He knew how to enter into the secret place with Hashem and listen to His heart. He was able to call upon the name of the Lord and focus intently on Him without getting distracted. David is an example of how we should enter into the spiritual holy of holies under our tallit. When you put the tallit over your head and bow down before Hashem, it is just you and Him—a true spiritual intimacy!

David *Hamelech* (King David) found the presence of the Lord in worship. Every time he entered the presence of Hashem and fell down on his face to experience God in the spiritual realm, he was able to behold the Teacher's face and see the beauty of our glorious Lord and King. This is why he could write, "ADONAI is my light and my salvation: whom should I fear? ADONAI is the stronghold of my life: whom should I dread?" (Ps. 27:1).

Within observant Jewish families, this verse from Psalm 27 is recited every day in the month of Elul, the month before the High Holidays, to help us prepare spiritually for the changes that will take place when Hashem shows us His light (Rosh Hashanah) and reveals to us His salvation (Yom Kippur). As we seek His presence and receive the blessings and benefits of spiritual intimacy with the Messiah, we come to realize that He has all the answers we will ever seek in our spiritual journey. They are given to us from one annual feast cycle to the next. All we have to do is receive them.

Imagine what David must have seen in the presence of Hashem to be able to say the following:

> When evildoers approached me to devour my flesh—
> my adversaries and my foes—they stumbled and fell.
> Though an army camp besieges me, my heart will
> not fear. Though war breaks out against me, even
> then will I be confident. One thing have I asked
> of ADONAI, that will I seek: to dwell in the House
> of ADONAI all the days of my life, to behold the
> beauty of ADONAI, and to meditate in His Temple.
> For in the day of trouble He will hide me in His

sukkah [shelter], conceal me in the shelter of His
tent, and set me high upon a rock.
—PSALM 27:2–5

David tasted everything a man could want in life:
wealth, power, authority, respect, and adulation. He was
surrounded by men who were willing to die for him, yet
he faced many enemies and battles throughout his life.
Negative spiritual forces constantly sought to destroy this
godly man. But David wasn't afraid because he was a worshipper. He was a praising man who thanked God for
all of his blessings! He was confident in God's grace and
mercy, and he knew the Lord would give him strength!

To have this kind of confidence, David longed for an
uninterrupted spiritual intimacy with his God. David saw
a splendor about Hashem that I have not seen yet in my
life. I have seen victories and I have seen miracles, but I
want to experience an uninterrupted spiritual intimacy
with my God like David had. My prayer is, "I want to see
Your face, Lord. I want to remain in Your presence!"

The presence of Hashem is always available to us. He
loves us and desires intimacy with us. That is why He
puts a longing to know Him in our hearts. And it is only
through a relationship with Yeshua that can we experience the fullness of what Hashem wants to give us.

David was willing to lay everything down on the altar
of sacrifice to dwell in the house of the Lord all the days of
his life. (See Psalm 27:4.) This is how he prayed:

Hear, ADONAI, when I call with my voice, be gracious
to me and answer me. To You my heart says: "Seek
My face." Your face, ADONAI, I seek. Do not hide

Your face from me. Do not turn Your servant away
in anger. You have been my help. Do not abandon
me or forsake me, O God my salvation. Though my
father and my mother forsake me, ADONAI will take
me in. Teach me Your way, ADONAI, and lead me on
a level path—because of my enemies. Do not turn
me over to the desire of my foes. For false witnesses
rise up against me breathing out violence. Surely I
trust that I will see the goodness of ADONAI in the
land of the living. Wait for ADONAI. Be strong, let
Your heart take courage, and wait for ADONAI.

—PSALM 27:7–14

To experience intimacy with Hashem, we must seek
Him! We must be willing to say to Yeshua, "Reveal Your-
self to me." Mankind was expelled from paradise, the Gan
Eden, because of our pride and lust. So in order to expe-
rience God's presence, we must be willing to lay down
our pride and self-reliance and totally submit ourselves to
Hashem. He far exceeds anything our minds can conceive.
The prophet Ezekiel described God's presence this way:

Above the expanse over their heads was something
like a throne, resembling a sapphire stone. Above the
shape of the throne was a figure of human appearance. From what appeared as his waist upward, I
saw a glowing metal, looking like a fire encased in
a frame. From what was like his waist down, I saw
the appearance of fire radiating around him. Like
the appearance of the rainbow in the cloud on a
rainy day, so was the appearance of the radiance. It
was the appearance of the likeness of the glory of

ADONAI. I saw it, fell upon my face, and heard the
voice of the One who was speaking.
—EZEKIEL 1:26–28

To experience the presence of the Teacher is an amazing
gift from Adonai, but we must learn how to receive it. We
must find a place where we can be alone with Him—a
secret place or a room in our homes where we can have
quiet and stillness. We need to be alone with Hashem at
a time and place when we can block out everything else.
We must be able to yield our thoughts, desires, emotions,
body, family, wealth, career, property, and the like to
Yeshua. When we do, we find that submission and obedience to Yeshua is a source of empowerment and freedom.
We become free from disorders, addictions, and fears, and
we receive the yoke of righteousness and eternal life.

Life in Yeshua is not about changing who we are but
about being changed into who we were meant to be. In
order to see this happen, we must align our will with His
will for us. Before we entered this path of spiritual pur-
suit and found the mystery of the prayer shawl and other
hidden treasures, our wrongdoings had been a betrayal to
the manifestation of the almighty God in our mortal flesh.
In the presence of Yeshua, the wrongs are forgiven.

As King David understood, true Jews are supposed to
worship the God of Israel. This should distinguish us from
the nations. We are supposed to be the voices lifting up
the authority of the Word of God and the reality of the
God of Abraham, Isaac, and Jacob. Today the whole body
of the Messiah should have this distinguishing feature.

Through worship, as we are covered with the tallit, we

learn to enter into the presence of God and experience His love. As we grow spiritually, our fears diminish and eventually depart because "there is no fear in love, but perfect love casts out fear, because fear has to do with punishment. Whoever fears is not perfect in love" (1 John 4:18, MEV). Today ask the Ruach to bring to the surface every fear that troubles or torments you. Confess any sins that are linked to those fears. Then ask Abba to replace those fears with His liberating love.

RUTH AND THE TALLIT

When we wrap ourselves in the tallit, we are symbolically wrapping ourselves in the Word of God. This allows us to encounter His presence. In the Old Testament, Ruth followed the exact instructions of her mother-in-law, Naomi, and went down to the threshing floor to lie at Boaz's feet. When he awoke, Boaz was startled to see a woman lying there. He questioned her to discover who she was and what she wanted. She identified herself as Ruth, his handmaid, and asked that he spread the corner of his garment (his tzitzit) over her because he was her *goel* (kinsman redeemer). In ancient Jewish and Middle Eastern culture, the spreading of the corner of the garment was a token of marriage.

By spreading his tallit over Ruth, Boaz was foreshadowing what the Messiah would do for us. Yeshua is our protection. When He spreads His tallit over us, we come under the covering of His protection. Just as Ruth, a Gentile, became Jewish by her obedience and faith in the

Word of God, so are we grafted into the family of Hashem when we obey and trust His Word.

HAMAKOM—"THE PLACE"

Instead of making our churches and synagogues places where we are comfortable, we should make them places where God feels at home. Another name for God is HaMakom, which is translated "the place." It comes from Genesis 28:16–17:

> Jacob woke up from his sleep and said, "Undoubtedly, ADONAI is in this place—and I was unaware." So he was afraid and said, "How fearsome this place is! This is none other than the House of God—this must be the gate of heaven!"

Jacob found himself at what is considered the holiest place in the universe—the place where the temple resided for almost a thousand years and where Abraham had been ready to surrender his beloved son, Isaac, who was Jacob's father. The manifest presence of God was visible in the place.

Rabbinic Midrash has spoken of the possibility that the stone Jacob took from the place and put under his head might have been the Foundation Stone of all creation—which is viewed in Jewish tradition as the spiritual junction of heaven and earth—because in his dream, "all of a sudden, there was a stairway set up on the earth and its top reaching to the heavens—and behold, angels of God going up and down on it!" (Gen. 28:12).

There are times in life when we become discouraged and despairing because our future seems uncertain. Our lives may seem to be falling apart as a result of wrong decisions we have made. There might be problems in our family or at our places of employment. We might be troubled about our financial needs or what seems to be a decline in our physical health. Whatever the concern, we should come close to Yeshua:

> Early in the morning Jacob got up and took the stone, which he had placed by his head, and set it up as a memorial stone and poured oil on top of it. He called the name of that place Beth-El [House of God].
>
> —GENESIS 28:18–19

Yeshua is the Place, and He is the stone upon which all creation has been founded. He is the Rock of all ages who can make right that which appears wrong. His presence appears at unexpected times and places because He is always with us and will never leave us or forsake us. His manifest presence may appear at good times when there is joy and success or at times of prayer and appreciation of the beauty of His creation. He may appear in times of study when we are on the verge of brilliant creativity or during challenging times when life never seems to get better.

Since we are all different in nature, background, education, and outlook, Yeshua customizes His appearance to each one of us to fit our unique circumstances. It is the Teacher's connection through His Spirit to our spirit (our inner essence) that enables us to experience His presence in our lives.

The key to experiencing the presence of God is to invite Him in to fellowship with us. But just as He appears at different times and different places, He reveals His presence to us in different ways. When Elijah was expecting God to appear, He was not in the great and mighty wind that was tearing at the mountains and shattering the cliffs, nor was His presence in the fire or the earthquake. It was, however, in the soft whisper of His voice. (See 1 Kings 19:11–12.)

We shouldn't be surprised to discover that the Teacher can appear to us whenever and wherever He chooses. He is the King! He is the Sovereign of the universe. There is no magic formula, chant, or object to rub to make Him appear. There is no checklist of rules and regulations that we must follow to win over His love and maintain His presence. His Word is a guide for us as a redeemed community. God's presence is a "banner [tallit] of love" over us (Song of Sol. 2:4). Nothing escapes His notice—not even the number of hairs on our head.

He is the Lord who is King, the Lord who was King, and the Lord who will always be King! His presence upon us is His love for us. His scepter is always extended for us to approach Him. (See Esther 8:4.) That is a perk we receive when we have an intimate relationship with Yeshua. As we spend time in His presence, He speaks to us through our minds, through our hearts, and through our spirits. He brings to mind verses He spoke to the prophets thousands of years ago, and in an instant those words bring special, personal meaning to each of us. This communication strengthens us to go forward as we are ever conscious that Yeshua is with us always.

If we have this consciousness of the Teacher with us, then why do we entertain thoughts of depression, fear, guilt, and insecurity? Where is our focus? Is it on Him or is it on the apparent circumstances in our lives? Our focus must be narrowed. Keeping our focus is a spiritual skill that has to be developed. We have to make a deliberate and conscious effort to stay on the path God has laid before us. When we allow ourselves to focus on all the destructive thoughts and problems that enter our minds, we lose our strength. Why do we allow them to rent free space in our heads? When we hand our concerns and problems over to God, He clears our minds and our whole outlook changes. The light of His presence fills us and we are revived. The joy of the Lord is our strength! Under the tallit we can get wonderfully lost in His intimate presence.

When we have Hashem's presence with us, it should be noticeable. When you have a closed bottle of exquisite-smelling perfume, it is like any other bottle. However, once it is opened, the magnificent aroma distinguishes it. When we know Yeshua and spend time with Him each day, His presence in our lives distinguishes us, and when people meet us, they should be able to ascertain His presence.

How do we become people distinguished by the presence of God or Shekinah? A person must desire to cleave to Him with all of his or her heart, mind, and spirit. We should be "weak with love," as the bridegroom expressed in Song of Solomon 2:5.

Yeshua in us is the hope of glory (Col. 1:27). As our eyes are opened to this truth, the blessing and realization of intimacy is awakened in our spirit. Through Yeshua, the *Etz Chayim* (Tree of Life), we can spiritually return to the Gan Eden, the garden of our King that is filled with spiritual delights for those who remain in His presence and who cultivate the garden according to His will.

SPIRITUAL AUTHORITY UNDER THE TALLIT

The tallit not only represents the presence of God but also the spiritual authority of Hashem. When *hasatan* (the devil) was cast down to the earth with the angels that followed him, it was because he rebelled against the authority of God. Rabbi Shaul tells us:

> Let every person submit himself to the governing authorities. For there is no authority except from God, and those that exist are put in place by God. So whoever opposes the authority has resisted God's direction, and those who have resisted will bring judgment on themselves. For leaders cause no fear for good behavior, but for bad. Now if you do not want to fear the authority, do what is good and you will get his approval—for he is God's servant to you for your good. But if you do evil, be afraid—for he does not carry the sword for no reason; for he is God's servant, an avenger who inflicts punishment on the evildoer. Therefore it is necessary to be in submission—not only because of punishment but also because of conscience. For this reason you also pay taxes, for the authorities are God's servants, attending diligently to this very thing. Pay

to everyone what is due them—tribute to whom
tribute is due; tax to whom tax is due; respect to
whom respect is due; honor to whom honor is due.

—ROMANS 13:1–7

When Eve listened to the serpent and went out from the
covering (tallit) of her husband, she went out from under
the covering (tallit) of God. When Adam also ate the fruit,
he too went out from under the covering (tallit) of God.
The result of disobeying spiritual authority is judgment,
and this judgment resulted in the fall of mankind. When
Hashem is no longer the top priority in your heart, you are
in rebellion. That is why Yeshua had to come on the scene.
All humankind was cast out of the Gan Eden, and there
was no way to return. The flaming swords of the cherubim
guarded the way to the Etz Chayim (Tree of Life).

Shame resulted from Adam and Eve's sin of rebellion. Once again, the rebellion took place when they gave
in to temptation and fell into the serpent's seductive trap.
Whenever we get out from under the authority of Hashem,
we make a statement to God that our needs and desires
take precedence over Him. There are only two paths we
can follow: the path to God or the path away from God.
He is a jealous God, and unbelief or anything that causes
us to remove ourselves from His authority will cause us
to reap judgment and shame. There is no possibility of
rebelling against God's authority without judgment! This
is why many believe it is important to wear the tallit katan
as protection against various tests of temptation in our
everyday lives.

God's authority represents God Himself. That is why it

is such a serious offense to defy God's authority. Rebellion is what led to Satan's fall. Satan wanted to exalt himself by setting his throne above God's throne, and this rebellion against God's authority is what God condemned when he cast Lucifer out of heaven.

> You were the seal of perfection, full of wisdom and perfect in beauty. You were in Eden, the garden of God. Every precious stone was your covering—ruby, topaz and diamond, beryl, onyx and jasper, sapphire, turquoise and emerald—your settings and your sockets a workmanship of gold—in the day you were created they were prepared. You were an anointed guardian *cheruv*. I placed you on the holy mountain of God. You walked among stones of fire. You were perfect in your ways from the day that you were created, until unrighteousness was found in you. By the abundance of your trade they filled you within with violence. So you have sinned. So I threw you out as a profane thing from the mountain of God. I made you vanish, guardian *cheruv* [cherub], from among the stones of fire. Your heart was exalted because of your beauty. You corrupted your wisdom because of your splendor. I threw you down to the earth.
>
> —EZEKIEL 28:12–17

None of us can ever comprehend God's ways. His ways are greater than our ways, and His thoughts are greater than our thoughts. In congregations there are always people vying for positions and favor. There are always people who love you until they are corrected. The insurgents are always prideful and arrogant. They may even have brilliant ideas and be extremely gifted and (unsurprisingly) creative, but almost always their hearts are the same as the one who was thrown out of heaven because he brought opposition to God's authority, which is opposition to God Himself.

The accuser is not as concerned with our preaching about Yeshua as he is with our submitting to the Teacher's authority, because if we are not under Yeshua's authority, our power is limited. Before he knew authority, Rabbi Shaul tried to wipe out the body of Messiah. But as Bible teacher Watchman Nee wrote, after he met the Lord on the road to Damascus in Acts 9, "he saw that it was hard for the feet (human power) to kick against the goads (God's authority)."[1]

Submitting to God's authority also extends to kingdom government. When we submit to a rabbi, pastor, or congregational leader, we are not subjecting ourselves to a person but to the anointing that is upon that person, the anointing given to him by God. Having said that, we should never be afraid to ask questions of our spiritual leaders. If they say something that doesn't line up with the Word of God, we should seek an explanation.

In my synagogue I encourage the members of the congregation to come see me if I say something they believe doesn't line up with the Word. I want to discuss it. If I am wrong, I will accept correction because I want to speak the word of the Lord, not the word of Charlie. I believe congregants should be able to trust their spiritual leaders; if they don't, they should be part of another congregation.

Our congregation is under the authority of a larger organization. We are people of authority under authority.

As followers of Hashem, we submit to God's authority by obeying His Word. Rebelling against Him brings serious consequences, as King Saul learned the hard way:

> "But I did obey the voice of ADONAI," Saul said to Samuel. "I went on the mission on which ADONAI sent me, and brought back Agag the king of Amalek—and utterly destroyed the Amalekites. But the people took some of the spoil, sheep and oxen— the best of what was under the ban of destruction— to sacrifice to ADONAI your God in Gilgal."
>
> Samuel said: "Does ADONAI delight in burnt offerings and sacrifices as in obeying the voice of ADONAI? Behold, to obey is better than sacrifice, to pay heed than the fat of rams. For rebellion is like the sin of divination and stubbornness is like iniquity and idolatry. Since you have rejected ADONAI's word, He has also rejected you as king."
>
> —1 SAMUEL 15:20–23

Yeshua would explain that even in sacrifice there is the element of self-will. In sacrifice and in self-denial there is still that flesh part of us that wants to give what we are comfortable giving and not necessarily the absolute best we can give. God wants us to give to Him the best and to have absolute trust in His ways.

We must continuously remember that we are not necessarily called to sacrifice and self-denial but to follow God's revealed purpose for us. In Matthew 7 we read about those who exercised much authority and used their spiritual gifts, including performing many miracles in Yeshua's name, yet they were reprimanded because they did it in the flesh and not according to the will of God (vv. 21–23). When everything you do points to you and not to Yeshua, you are trying to rob Him of the glory.

Once again, Yeshua looks at the heart. The two main principles of spiritual authority are trust and obedience. We would be wise to ask Hashem to reveal to us any ways we may have removed ourselves from God's authority, and then immediately repent of this serious sin of rebelling against God's authority. What a blessing that we have such a great Teacher who loves us unconditionally and will forgive us when we confess and turn away from our sin.

WEARING THE TALLIT IN HUMILITY

Because when we wrap ourselves in the tallit, we are symbolically wrapping ourselves in the presence of God, it should never be our ambition to use the tallit to make ourselves seem more holy or spiritual. That is what the Pharisees did, and Yeshua condemned them harshly, saying:

> All their works they do to be noticed by men. They make their *tefillin* [phylacteries or Scripture boxes] wide and their *tzitziyot* [tassels] long. They love the place of honor at feasts, the best seats in the synagogues, greetings in the marketplaces, and to be called rabbi by men...Woe to you, *Torah* scholars and Pharisees, hypocrites! You clean the outside of

the cup and dish, but inside they are full of greed
and uncontrolled desire. O blind Pharisee! First
clean the inside of the cup and dish, so that the outside may become clean as well.

—MATTHEW 23:5–7, 25–26

We are to wear the tallit in humility, seeking to bring
glory to Yeshua and not to ourselves. Our carnal nature is
all about "me" or "I," but when we humble ourselves before
Yeshua, our concern is all about Him, our eternal source.
Humility is a fruit of the Spirit. It comes from Yeshua.
Pride, conversely, comes from our flesh nature. Pride is
divisive and causes separation, while humility heals and
brings reconciliation.

Pride led to Lucifer's fall from heaven, and it has influ-
enced mankind since the Gan Eden. We have taken the
attitude that we can rise to the top on our own. But the
more we seek to ascend to higher levels of wisdom, knowledge, riches, greatness, reputation, beauty, and happiness,
the emptier we become. Following any plan other than
the Teacher's leads to a life without true meaning. Seeking
Hashem—and not our own advancement—under the tallit
will remind us to humbly submit to Yeshua's will and not
pursue our own!

In Noah's day, humankind strayed appallingly from
the way of Adonai. (See Genesis 6.) When one strays
from God, it means he is following the ways of the flesh,
which is the way of pride, lust, and selfish ambition. Following Yeshua in an intimate relationship through His
Word and following the ways of the world will each leave

an imprint. We have to choose which impression we want to represent us.

Noah chose the way of the Teacher and found favor in the eyes of Hashem (Gen. 6:8). Noah was a righteous man who walked with God, but his righteousness alone could not have saved him. He was saved due to God's unmerited (or free) favor. Noah experienced this unmerited favor because he submitted to Hashem by humbling himself and following God's instructions and not simply exalting himself.

How then do you find favor in the eyes of Adonai? Through faith and humility. Humility is walking according to the will of God. "Though He scoffs at the scoffers, He gives grace to the humble" (Prov. 3:34).

The battle between the *yetzer hara* (the evil inclination) and the *yetzer hatov* (the good inclination) has been ongoing since the Garden of Eden. It is the battle between the evil one and the Spirit of the Mighty One of Israel. This seduction of mankind has persisted since the Gan Eden. However, when Yeshua came to this earth and successfully finished His work on the tree by dying and rising again, He won the victory over sin!

In ancient Babylon "the entire earth had the same language with the same vocabulary" (Gen. 11:1). Can you imagine how powerful the people of the earth could have been if they had not given in to the temptation from yetzer hara and from hasatan and instead had humbly submitted to Yeshua? He could have exalted them to magnificence. But they yielded to seduction:

Then they said, "Come! Let's build ourselves a city, with a tower whose top reaches into heaven. So let's make a name for ourselves, or else we will be scattered over the face of the whole land."

Then ADONAI came down to see the city and the tower that the sons of man had built. ADONAI said, "Look, the people are one and all of them have the same language. So this is what they have begun to do. Now, nothing they plan to do will be impossible. Come! Let Us go down and confuse their language there, so that they will not understand each other's language."

So ADONAI scattered them from there over the face of the entire land, and they stopped building the city. This is why it is named Babel, because ADONAI confused the languages of the entire world there, and from there ADONAI scattered them over the face of the entire world.

—GENESIS 11:4–9

We must take a good look at ourselves and take an account. Instead of seeking to exalt ourselves, we need to be just like Yeshua. He did not rise to greatness; He descended to greatness. "Though existing in the form of God, [the Teacher] did not consider being equal to God a thing to be grasped. But He emptied Himself—taking on the form of a slave, becoming the likeness of men and being found in appearance as a man. He humbled Himself" (Phil. 2:6–8).

Pride and arrogance have the ability to spiritually blind you in such a way that your heart becomes hardened, sometimes to the point of no return. We must consider our ways. Do I have a humble heart? Do I guard my heart to make sure the flesh does not hinder my relationship with Yeshua? The mind affects our thinking, but the heart affects our destiny! When we stand with the tallit around us, are we cleansed and purified or are we holding on to some type of sin? Yes, we are cleansed and purified by the Messiah's blood, but are we like David, who had to be confronted in order to realize he needed to repent of his sin with Bathsheba? (See 2 Samuel 12.) Have we come under the tallit knowing that we have offended someone and have not asked forgiveness?

What kind of hearts does God want His children to have? "The sacrifices of God are a broken spirit; a broken and a contrite heart, O God, You will not despise" (Ps. 51:17, MEV).

We are able to walk in humility and submit our ambitions to Yeshua when we know we are loved. Without love, we feel unimportant and unproductive in life. Then we begin to compare ourselves with others—our looks, our abilities, our accomplishments, and our wealth or power. Instead of humility, we develop covetousness and lust, which is a manifestation of pride.

I was blessed to have parents who loved me and told me they were proud of me. When you experience love from your natural father, it is easier to experience love from your heavenly Father. But as followers of Yeshua, no matter what we have experienced in the past, we must realize that we worship a God who sacrificed Himself for us so we could spend eternity with Him. That is an amazing love! And what does He expect from us in return? "Only that you remain in awe [reverential fear] of God your Lord, so that you will follow all His paths and love Him, serving God your Lord with all your heart and with all your soul. You must keep God's commandments and decrees…so that good will be yours" (Deut. 10:12–13).[2]

The tallit is a holy object, and those who wear it must walk humbly before God. Humbling ourselves before Yeshua is a process, but if we seek Hashem in prayer and even fasting, He will purify our hearts. Humbling ourselves before Yeshua will only bring us into a deeper relationship with Him.

Throughout this chapter, we have seen that the tallit symbolizes the covering, presence, and authority of God. We cannot even fathom how much He desires to love, protect, and fellowship with us. It is hard for any of us to imagine the effulgence of His glory. It is thought that, like in the Book of Esther where God's name is never mentioned, there is a "hiddenness" in the presence of God. However, when we receive that kesher (connection) to the divine through Yeshua, we are blessed to be able to experience the manifest presence of Hashem. He is from antiquity—always was, always is, and always will be.

CHAPTER 4

YESHUA AND THE TALLIT: HEALING IN HIS WINGS

EVERYTHING ABOUT EXPERIENCING the mystery of the prayer shawl points to Yeshua, the Teacher. The tallit is all about Him. It represents the Word of God, and He is the Living Word. It is most likely that Yeshua always wore a tallit because doing so was required by the Torah and He obeyed the Law of Moses. But there was something special about the Teacher's tallit. In the Word of God, we see instances of people reaching out to take hold of the hem of His garment, the tzitzit, so they would be healed. This was a profound, faith-filled act that, as we will see in this chapter, confirmed that Yeshua was indeed the promised Messiah.

The Scriptures tell us:

> But for you who revere My Name, the sun of righteousness will rise, with healing in its wings.
>
> —MALACHI 3:20
> (MALACHI 4:2 IN SOME TRANSLATIONS)

The *sun of righteousness* has been interpreted to mean the Messiah, and the Hebrew term for *wings* is *kanaph* or *kanaphecha*. Consequently, the verse has been interpreted to read, "When the Messiah arises there will be healing through His *kanaph* or tzitzit, the corner of His tallit." This is why those who were ill wanted to grab the corner of Yeshua's garment, the tzitzit, which represents the Word of God. They believed that Yeshua was the Messiah and that there was healing in His "wings."

We read in the Book of Matthew:

> Just then a woman, losing blood for twelve years, came from behind and touched the *tzitzit* of His

garment. For she kept saying to herself, "If only I touch His garment, I will be healed."

But then *Yeshua* turned and saw her. "Take heart, daughter," He said, "your faith has made you well." That very hour the woman was healed.

—MATTHEW 9:20–22

I recall with fond memories that, when I was ten years old, my parents took me to see the movie *Ben Hur* at Radio City Music Hall. What stood out to me was that this Messiah had multitudes and multitudes of followers wherever He journeyed, and those He touched were healed. The movie was actually showing me the fulfillment of Yeshua's Word:

And when the men of that place recognized *Yeshua*, they sent word into all the surrounding region. And they brought to Him all those who were in bad shape and kept begging Him that they might just touch the *tzitzit* of His garment—and all who touched it were cured.

—MATTHEW 14:35–36

Of course, I had no idea what that passage said because as a young Jewish boy growing up in the United States in post-Holocaust times, I was never taught about Yeshua. I had no idea the garment He was wearing was a tallit katan, a garment that contained the tzitzit or the kanaph, and that there is healing through the power of His Word.

Still today healing comes through the power of the Word. While Adonai Himself is the One who heals—His name is *Adonai Rofecha*, "the LORD your Healer" (Exod. 15:26)—He does so through the Word of God.

We see even in the Tanakh that healing comes through the Word of God. Consider this example from the life of the prophet Elijah:

> It came to pass that the son of the woman, the mistress of the house fell sick, and his sickness was getting much worse until he had no breath left in him. So she said to Elijah, "What do I have to do with you, man of God? Have you come to me to remind me of my sin and kill my son?"
>
> He said to her, "Give me your son." Then he took him from her arms, carried him up to the upper room where he was staying and laid him on his own bed. He cried out to ADONAI and said, "ADONAI my God, have You brought such evil even on the widow with whom I am staying, by causing her son to die?" Then he stretched himself upon the child three times. He cried out to ADONAI and said, "ADONAI my God, please let this child's soul come back into his body!"
>
> ADONAI listened to the cry of Elijah, so the soul of the child came back into his body and he was revived. Then Elijah took the child and brought him down from the upper room into the house, and gave him to his mother. Elijah said, "See! Your son is alive."
>
> Then the woman said to Elijah, "Now I know that you are a man of God, and that the word in your mouth is truth."
>
> —1 KINGS 17:17–24

In this passage we see that Elijah went to the widow's house, carried her dead son to the upper room where he was staying, and laid him on his own bed. Then he stretched himself on the child three times while wearing his tallit and cried out to Adonai to heal the child. How do we know Elijah was wearing his tallit? Because healing is by the Word of God, which is represented by the tzitzit.

In the B'rit Chadashah (New Testament), people were healed when Yeshua spoke the Word of God and when they touched the hem (tzitzit) of His garment. When a man with *tza'arat* (leprosy) came to the Teacher begging Him to make him clean, Yeshua was moved with compassion, stretched out His hand, and healed him, possibly by touching him with the tzitzit. There is a healing anointing that comes through the tzitzit, but that healing comes because of Hashem's desire to heal, not because of the tzitzit or any other holy object.

Hashem's desire to heal us is one of the major hidden treasures that we discover as we experience the mystery of the prayer shawl. In Psalm 17:8, David cried, "Hide me in the shadow of Your wings." The four corners of the tallit are the "corners of the garment" or the "wings" or the "skirt" or the "robe" that brings healing to those who dwell under the shadow of His wings. We also see this truth in Psalm 91, where Yeshua promises to protect us from the deadly pestilence. He declares that He will cover us with His feathers and under His wings we will find refuge. He tells us not to fear the plague that stalks in darkness. Though a thousand may fall at our side and ten thousand at our right hand, it will not come near us. He promises that no evil will befall us nor will any plague come near to our dwelling. Then He ends the psalm by saying, "With long life will I satisfy him and show him My salvation" (Ps. 91:16).

Hashem promises us long life! Healing is an amazing gift that has always been there for us to receive. Yeshua voluntarily did this for us: "Surely He has borne our griefs and carried our pains. Yet we esteemed Him stricken, struck by God, and afflicted. But He was pierced because of our transgressions, crushed because of our iniquities. The chastisement for our *shalom* [peace] was upon Him, and by His stripes we are healed" (Isa. 53:4–5).

How can we thank Yeshua for this treasure? He says that if we love Him, we will follow His commandments.

In the story of the woman with the blood flow for twelve years, we read that Yeshua felt power going out from Him after the woman touched the fringes (tzitzit) of His tallit (Luke 8:46). Another hidden treasure in the mystery of the prayer shawl is the power of God working through you to pray for and experience incredible healing for yourself and others. However, when we read the account of how the healing power of God went out from Yeshua and entered the woman so she could be healed, a possible problem arises.

Leviticus 15:19 tells us that a woman who had a discharge of blood from her body would be considered unclean for a period of seven days, and anyone or anything that touched her would be unclean until the evening. Also, any man who lay with her during the time of *niddah* (ritual state of being unclean) would also be unclean for seven days. So how could Yeshua, who lived a perfect, sinless life, continue on to Jairus's house to heal his daughter after having been touched by a ritually unclean woman? I believe the answer to that question is found in the heading before that passage in my Bible, which is the Tree of Life Version. It says Jesus was "Interrupted on the Way to a Miracle":

> As *Yeshua* returned, the crowd welcomed Him, for they were all expecting Him. And here came a man named Jairus, a leader in the synagogue. Falling at *Yeshua's* feet, he begged Him to come to his house, because his only daughter, about twelve years old, was dying. But as He made His way, the masses were crushing in upon Him.
>
> And there was a woman with a blood flow for twelve years, who could not be healed by anyone. She came up from behind and touched the *tzitzit* of *Yeshua's* garment. Immediately, her blood flow stopped. *Yeshua* said, "Who touched Me?"
>
> When everyone denied it, Peter said, "Master, the crowds are surrounding You and pressing in!"
>
> But *Yeshua* said, "Someone touched Me, for I recognized power going out from Me." Then seeing that she did not escape notice, the woman came trembling and fell prostrate before Him. In the presence of all the people, she confessed why she had touched Him and how she had been healed immediately. He said to her, "Daughter, your faith has made you well. Go in *shalom*."
>
> While He was still speaking, someone comes from the house of the synagogue leader, saying, "Your daughter has died. Don't bother the Teacher anymore."

But hearing this, *Yeshua* replied to him, "Do not fear—just keep trusting, and she shall be restored."

When *Yeshua* came into the house, He didn't let anyone enter with Him except Peter, John, Jacob, and the child's father and mother. And everyone was weeping and lamenting her; but He said, "Don't weep, for she didn't die but is sleeping." But they were ridiculing Him, knowing she had died.

But *Yeshua*, took her by the hand and called out, saying, "Child, get up!" Her spirit returned, and she arose immediately.

—LUKE 8:40–55

How could Jesus have touched Jairus's daughter and healed her when He was ceremonially unclean because the woman with the issue of blood had touched Him? The answer could be that when Jesus was "interrupted on the way to a miracle"—when the incident took place with the woman with the issue of the blood—it was at the point that Jairus's daughter died. Perhaps the miracle Adonai had determined to show was greater than healing the woman with the issue of blood—it was to resurrect a young girl from the dead. Revealing His resurrection power was more important than debates over His cleanliness or uncleanliness.

It is also believed that the child was healed after being wrapped in the tallit. Some scholars say that when Yeshua said, "Child, get up!" He was actually saying in Aramaic, "Child wrapped in the tallit, get up!" Yeshua would have spoken both Hebrew and Aramaic, and the child could have already been wrapped in a tallit to prepare her for burial, which is customary. This is more speculation than fact, but it is an interesting idea. It would make sense because Yeshua was that Unique Individual of whom John wrote:

> In the beginning was the Word. The Word was with God, and the Word was God. He was with God in the beginning. All things were made through Him, and apart from Him nothing was made that has come into being… And the Word became flesh and tabernacled among us. We looked upon His glory, the glory of the one and only from the Father, full of grace and truth.
>
> —JOHN 1:1–3, 14

The healing of Jairus's daughter is yet another example of healing taking place through the manifest presence of God and the miraculous power of His Word. The Bible is filled with miracles and healings from the beginning in *Bereishit* (Genesis) to the last Book, the Revelation. Many of those miraculous healings took place so Adonai could prove that Yeshua was indeed the Messiah.

MESSIANIC MIRACLES

The love Hashem has for us is unimaginable! He absolutely wants us to depend upon Him so He can take care of us. He communicates this love to us through His Book, the Bible. He shows us miracles so we will know that He is greater than nature or anything that occurs in the natural. He heals so we will truly understand that He alone is victorious over every disease. He shows His compassion for us and tells us to not let our hearts be troubled. He wants us to live in Him, which is to live in everlasting peace.

Modern medicine has shown that, when our hearts and minds are troubled and filled with stress and worry, our resistance to disease is lower and the quivers of sickness and affliction can attack us. This is why Yeshua tells us to guard our hearts and minds by trusting in Him (Phil. 4:7). When a person places the tallit upon his head so he may enter his prayer closet, and when he grabs the tzitzit and calls out to the Teacher for healing, he is demonstrating strong faith in the One who heals! His finished work on the tree (cross) has brought us healing, forgiveness, restoration, justification, and reconciliation. When we stand in faith, fear departs and we can walk in the authority of the Ruach HaKodesh with power, love, and a sound mind.

As our hearts and minds are healed, our bodies heal also. Rabbi Alfred J. Kotlatch noted that "Judaism rejects the idea that the laws of nature can be contravened. As far back as Talmudic times, rabbis expressed opinions that the miracles of the Bible were not breaks with nature but events programmed into nature at the time of Creation." It is believed by most rabbis and Jewish philosophers throughout the ages that God Himself would not want to interfere with His natural laws.[1]

I am Jewish. I was born and raised as a Jew. I had my circumcision (bris or brit) on the eighth day, I had my bar mitzvah at the age of thirteen, and I was married as a Jew in a Jewish ceremony. I now live as a Jew in more traditional and observant ways than I ever had previously practiced. I have always believed and, of course, still do believe that there is only one God!

I also have always believed that Hashem is the Creator of the universe and all that exists. The miracles that are written in the Bible were performed only through the power of God! I believe that the one God of the Bible, who programmed events into nature at the time of Creation, could have miraculously programmed Himself to be simultaneously God the Father on the throne and the Messiah on the earth.

Mankind is inventing, discovering, and advancing all fields at a greater pace than at any other time in history. Our society is in the midst of an astronomical intellectual progression that could possibly be the beginning of its downfall. Is it possible that we can believe mankind can do more and more but God's power is limited? God's power hasn't changed. Scripture is filled with stories of Yeshua healing the sick, blind, and hurting, proving again and again that He is the Messiah. If He did it then, He can still heal today.

HEALING THE MAN BORN BLIND

One of my favorite stories about the Teacher's miraculously healing someone is when He was just passing by and saw a man who had been blind since birth. People had been healed from blindness, but only the Messiah could heal someone who was born blind. It was believed that for a person to be born blind, either the person or his parents had to have sinned. Yet Yeshua declared that "Neither this man nor his parents sinned. This happened so that the works of God might be brought to light in him" (John 9:3). In this account the Teacher also declared that

He was the Messiah by saying, "I am the light of the world" (John 9:5).

Again, only God would be the light of the world, and Scripture declares that God and the Messiah are one! Each time Yeshua healed a person, He used a different creative method to perform the miracle. This was to show that He is in control of everything in nature and He can do whatever He and the Father decide. (Remember, they are one!) This time He spit on the ground, made mud with the saliva, and spread the mud on the blind man's eyes. Then He told him, "Go, wash in the Pool of Siloam" (John 9:7). When the man returned, he miraculously could see.

The people who knew him, his neighbors and friends, were startled. "It looks like him," they must have said, "but it can't be him. It's impossible! He was blind from birth! How did this happen?" The man responded by telling them what Yeshua had done and said. Still not able to believe what they were seeing, they took the man before the ruling Pharisees. When the Pharisees asked him how he was healed, he responded the same way with the same story, but they didn't believe him. It was Shabbat, which meant Yeshua couldn't be the Messiah because everyone knew you can't heal on Shabbat. It's against rabbinic law!

Others, however, said that a sinner could not perform such miraculous signs (John 9:16). They asked the man what he had to say about the one who healed him, and the man said, "He's a prophet" (John 9:17). The Judean leaders still did not believe him. They thought that maybe the man hadn't been born blind, so they asked his parents. But his parents feared the leaders, who had already agreed that anyone who professed that Yeshua was the Messiah would be thrown out of the synagogue. So they said, "We know that this is our son and that he was born blind. We don't know how he now sees, nor do we know who opened his eyes" (John 9:20–21). Subsequently, they told the leaders to ask their son because he was old enough to speak for himself. Once again they asked the once-blind man the same set of questions. This time he said he didn't care whether the one who healed him was a sinner or not because he was born blind and he could now see!

The Pharisees kept pressing him, wanting to know what Yeshua had done to him. Frustrated because they didn't believe what he told them, the man sarcastically asked if they too were interested in becoming one of His disciples, to which they fulminated against him. (See John 9:26–28.)

The religious leaders may have tried to deny it, but their efforts were futile. Only the Messiah could heal someone who was born blind. By performing this miracle, Yeshua was confirming His identity as the One whose power is not limited. He is still able to do exceedingly abundantly above all that we could ask or think (Eph. 3:20–21).

One year while my wife and I were praying for people at the Messiah Conference in Grantham, Pennsylvania, a woman approached us. She was an author, and her doctors had said she was losing her sight and would end up legally blind. This had been occurring for some time, and not much could be done to help her. I told her that as a retired optometrist, I would call out and pray for every structure of her eyes to be healed. The next morning my wife ran into her and again prayed for her. She told Racquel that when we prayed for her the previous night, she just believed that God would heal her.

Years passed, and we forgot about that situation. Then one day we received a package in the mail. It was from the woman for whom we prayed. She asked if we remembered her and told us that she had indeed been healed and that she was sending us two books she had written after her healing.

Yeshua does work miracles, and it is our job to pray for people with confidence, knowing that it is not about us or what we pray, but it is all about Him and His will being fulfilled! When we grab onto the fringes of the tallit, we are declaring that we believe in Yeshua's Word and that we can be touched by Hashem and healed!

HEALING THE LEPER

Another Messianic miracle Yeshua performed was the healing of a Jewish leper. No Jewish person had been healed of leprosy (*tza'arat*) until Yeshua performed this miracle. (In the Tanakh, Naaman was healed of leprosy, but he was the commander of the army of the king of Aram.) We read in Luke's Gospel:

> Now while *Yeshua* was in one of the towns, a man covered with [*tza'arat*] appeared. And when he saw *Yeshua*, he fell on his face and begged Him, saying, "Master, if You are willing, You can make me clean."
>
> *Yeshua* stretched out His hand and touched him, saying, "I am willing. Be cleansed!" Immediately, the [*tza'arat*] left him. *Yeshua* ordered him to tell no one, but commanded him, "Go and show yourself to the *kohen*. Then bring an offering for your

cleansing, just as Moses commanded, as a testimony to them."

—LUKE 5:12–14

Let's not forget that Yeshua was wearing His tallit katan at that time. We know this because He wore it every day. This miracle was accomplished so that Hashem would receive the glory. Yeshua told the man to show himself to the priest (kohen), as the Torah instructed::

> Then *ADONAI* spoke to Moses and to Aaron saying: "When a man has a swelling on the skin of his body or a scab or a bright spot, and it becomes the plague-mark of *tza'arat* in his flesh, then he should be brought to Aaron the *kohen*, or to one of his sons, the *kohanim*."
>
> —LEVITICUS 13:1–2

> Then *ADONAI* spoke to Moses, saying: "This is the *Torah* of the one with *tza'arat* in the day of his cleansing. He should be brought to the *kohen*, and the *kohen* is to go to the outside of the camp. The *kohen* is to examine him, and behold, if the mark of *tza'arat* is healed in one with *tza'arat*, then the *kohen* is to command that two clean living birds, cedar wood, scarlet and hyssop be brought for the one being cleansed."
>
> —LEVITICUS 14:1–4

We don't know how the *kohanim* (priests) reacted to the leper being healed, but I'm sure it was much like the Judean leaders' reaction after the Jewish man who had been born blind was healed. How could this sinner heal a Jewish person of *tza'arat*? Only the Messiah could do that!

HEALING THE DEMON-POSSESSED

Most people who believe in God also believe there are spiritual beings we can't see. This is why people search for life's meaning. They want to know about the things we don't see. People are searching for answers that can be ascertained. In the days of antiquity, people were more aware of angels and demons. The angels, of course, were always a blessing, but the demons needed to be cast out.

The Messiah demonstrated His spiritual authority by speaking to the demon inside of someone and causing it to leave the person. This is what He did for a demon-possessed man who was blind and mute.

> Then a demon-plagued man, who was blind and mute, was brought to *Yeshua*; and He healed him, so that he spoke and saw. All the crowds were astounded and saying, "This can't be *Ben-David*, can it?"
>
> —MATTHEW 12:22–23

But it was Ben-David, the Son of David (another title for the Messiah). Only the Messiah could accomplish such a miracle. Most of the Pharisees, of course, rejected this healing because they did not believe Yeshua was the Messiah. Instead of embracing the truth of who the Teacher was, they proclaimed that He was driving out the demons by Beelzebul (Satan), the ruler of demons. Yeshua responded to this by saying, "Every kingdom divided against itself is destroyed, and every city or house divided against itself will not stand" (Matt. 12:25).

He then asked them, "If I drive out demons by *beelzebul*, by whom do your sons drive them out?" This question made sense. However, He continued: "if I drive out demons by the *Ruach Elohim*, then the kingdom of God has come upon you" (Matt. 12:28). Everything Yeshua did was to reveal who He was and to bring glory to God the Father.

HEALING LAZARUS

Yeshua had an inner circle of people who followed Him and were with Him when He accomplished miracles that only the Messiah could perform. One family that was close to Him included Miriam (Mary), the one who had anointed Yeshua with oil and wiped His feet with her hair (John 11:2); Martha, the one with the gift of serving; and Lazarus, the close friend for whom Yeshua wept. When Lazarus was sick to the point of death, his sisters asked Yeshua to come quickly so their brother could be healed. But when Yeshua heard the news, He knew the sickness would bring glory to the *Ben Elohim*, the Son of God. (Because Yeshua and God are one, all the glory that goes to Yeshua goes to God.) Consequently, He stayed where He was for two more days, and during that time Lazarus died. By the time Yeshua arrived at his friends' home, Lazarus had been buried in the tomb for four days.

Judeans came from all over to console Martha and Miriam. Martha saw Yeshua and protested that, if He had come earlier, her brother would not have died. To that He replied, "Your brother will rise again" (John 11:23). Again, she protested that she knew her brother would rise in the resurrection (Jewish people have always believed that there will be a resurrection of the dead), but had Yeshua come sooner, he would still be alive. Yeshua then responded, "I am the resurrection and the life! Whoever believes in Me, even if he dies, shall live. And whoever lives and believes in Me shall never die" (John 11:25–26). After He spoke those words, He asked Martha if she believed what He said. She answered, "Yes, Lord, I believe that you are the Messiah, *Ben Elohim* who has come into the world" (John 11:27).

Miriam then came to see Yeshua and also protested His delayed arrival by saying, "Master, if You had been here, my brother would not have died!" (John 11:32). When Yeshua saw Miriam and all the other Judeans weeping, He wept too. They all realized how much Yeshua loved Lazarus. Many were puzzled, wondering why the One who opened the eyes of the man born blind could not have kept Lazarus from dying.

Yeshua proceeded to go to the tomb to see Lazarus. Martha again protested when He asked that the stone be rolled away, declaring that her brother had been dead for four days and the tomb would stink. Nevertheless, Yeshua was again allowing this for the glory of God, which was revealed when He said, "Didn't I tell you that if you believed, you would see the glory of God?" (John 11:40). Yeshua then called Lazarus to come forth from the grave, and he did. And he wasn't a mummy or a zombie; Lazarus was alive!

By performing this miracle, Yeshua did something the Judeans and Pharisees knew could only be accomplished by the Messiah. In the days of antiquity, people had been resurrected but never anyone who had been in the tomb for more than three days. Only the Messiah could resurrect someone who had been dead for four days!

HEALING THE PARALYZED MAN

At another time a group of people brought to Yeshua a paralyzed man lying on a cot. Yeshua saw their faith and told the man that his sins were forgiven. Some of the Torah scholars heard Yeshua's words and thought what He said was blasphemy because only God or the Messiah, who is God, has the authority to forgive sins. (See Matthew 9:1–3.) Yeshua then used a principle called *kal va-chomer*, which is used throughout the whole Bible but was first written down by Rabbi Hillel before the common era in his seven rules of hermeneutics. *Kal va-chomer* is a logical deduction process. It says, for example, that if I can do the first thing, then how much greater would it be if I could do the second thing, which is more difficult?

We see this process in Matthew 9:5 when Yeshua asked, "Which is easier, to say, 'Your sins are forgiven,' or to say, 'Get up and walk'?" Obviously, it is easier to say that your sins are forgiven because no one would really know if they were or not. However, how much greater would it be for Yeshua to tell the man to take up his mat and walk? If the man could not do it, Yeshua would not be who He was proclaiming to be. If He did the more difficult thing, He could certainly do the simpler thing. As we know, the man did get healed. He took up his mat and walked, and once again Yeshua proved that He was the Messiah and gave all the glory to God!

YESHUA IS STILL THE HEALER

God is a healer, but He wants us to maintain a healthy lifestyle. Daniel, for example, changed his diet and his way of living to remain in good health and in excellent spirit while he was living in exile in Babylon. We too may be called upon to make changes in our diet and way of living to stay in good health (or to reclaim good health) so we can be strong enough to fulfill God's purpose for our lives.

There are times, however, when God allows us to go through health trials to build our faith in His power to heal and provide for us. Whenever we are facing a health trial, we should see it as God does and "consider it all joy…knowing that the testing of your faith produces endurance" (Jacob [James] 1:2–3).

A business acquaintance of mine once told me that his wife had been sick with stomach problems for over a year. She had been to different doctors, but she could not be healed. She was often in excruciating pain. We were having a special healing service, and I sensed the Ruach Elohim tell me to call the man and invite his wife to our services. I told him that I really believed Hashem was going to do something special.

The man convinced his wife to attend, but at the last minute she was in such terrible pain that she felt she couldn't make it. When he called to tell me, I told him to try to get her there as best he could. Miraculously her pain subsided enough for her to attend with him. During the service I covered her with the tallit I was wearing, and my wife and I prayed for her. Immediately she felt better, but she worried about how she might feel in the morning.

She went to sleep and woke up the next morning with no pain, and she never again had that condition. This was about seven or eight years ago. We've seen Yeshua work through us to heal many different types of afflictions through the years.

Just as the Messiah had the authority to heal through His Word, so do we as His children. He gave His disciples authority to heal the sick (Matt. 10:1, 8; Luke 9:1; 10:9), and as His children we have that authority too. We can pray for the sick with confidence, knowing that God desires that we be in good health (3 John 2) and that by His stripes we *were* healed (Isa. 53:5; 1 Pet. 2:24). That means the provision for our healing has already been made!

When you wrap the tallit around a person, ask him to grab the tzitzit in faith, and pray for that person's healing, you and that individual need to expect that Hashem will do something miraculous. However, we must remember that God is on the throne, and He can heal whom He wants to heal in whatever way He chooses to do so. Yet we stand a better chance of seeing God do the miraculous if we pray for healing with steadfast faith in His power and His Word.

In Isaiah 38, we read that Hezekiah, one of the greatest kings of Israel, had become mortally ill. Adonai told him through the prophet Isaiah that he should put his house in order because he was going to die. When he heard the news, King Hezekiah immediately began to pray. Weeping bitterly, he pleaded with the Lord, reminding Him of how he had walked before Him in truth with his whole heart. After a short time Adonai spoke to Isaiah and told him to tell Hezekiah that He had heard his prayers and would allow him to live another fifteen years. When we pray with *kavanah* (with intention from the bottom of one's heart), God hears us and responds!

If we desire to experience healing from the Teacher, we must have faith in His Word. We must not only hear the Word of Yeshua but also believe it. When we really believe God's Word deep within, God is able to perform miraculous healings in and through us. If we were very sick, even to the point of being near death, and were told that a certain medication might help us, there is no question that we would find it, pay whatever price was required, and take the medicine for as long as it was needed. The same must be true of spiritual medicine.

If we truly believe Yeshua's Word, we will pray, intercede, and battle in the spirit realm for hours, days, or even months to receive the breakthrough and victory. God does use the brilliance of modern medicine and therapeutic treatment regimens, but many times the fullness of healing comes with a victorious battle in the spirit realm through prayer and faith.

If you or a loved one is suffering with an affliction, battle in the spirit realm for healing. Put on your tallit, grab hold of the tzitzit, and pray with strong faith. Then watch and see the fruit of trusting God's Word!

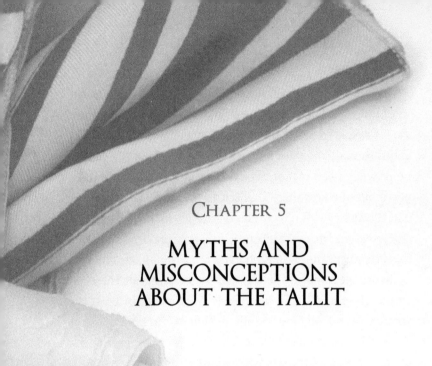

CHAPTER 5

MYTHS AND
MISCONCEPTIONS
ABOUT THE TALLIT

OR ALL THE amazing spiritual truths revealed in the tallit, there are also many myths and misconceptions associated with it. Some of the stories circulating about the tallit are not actually false—they simply cannot be proven, and for that reason I classify them as myths. I personally believe there is merit to some of the claims we will discuss in this chapter, and I sometimes refer to those stories when I teach. However, I always make it clear that the stories are quite possibly true but are not settled fact.

So as we explore the following stories about the tallit, let us remember that a believer in Messiah must trust the written Word of God as the authority for truth. Everything else takes second place. There can be no compromise in this. We can consider these stories and even personally believe they may be true, but we cannot allow commentaries or religious tradition to take precedence over what Hashem has said. With that understanding, let us begin.

THE TALLIT AS
THE LIGHT OF GOD

Yeshua's presence is effulgent. The more we live in Hashem's holy presence, the more His resplendent radiance shines forth from us. Scripture says, "God is light and in Him there is no darkness at all. If we say we have fellowship with Him and keep walking in the darkness, we are lying and do not practice the truth. But if we walk in the light as He Himself is in the light, we have fellowship with one another" (1 John 1:5–7). And "in Him was life, and the life was the light of men. The light shines in the darkness, and the darkness has not overpowered it" (John 1:4–5).

Because of this, some have said that God puts on a tallit as we do, but His tallit is His light.

It has been said that the light of God is the tallit of God because the psalmist says He is "clothed with splendor and majesty—wrapping [Himself] in light as a robe, stretching out heaven like a curtain" (Ps. 104:1–2). According to this view, the light of the tallit that was wrapped around Him was the light of all creation, and all things were created through this light. Colossians 1:15–19 is often used to support this claim:

> He is the image of the invisible God, the firstborn of all creation. For by Him all things were created— in heaven and on earth, the seen and the unseen, whether thrones or angelic powers or rulers or authorities. All was created through Him and for Him. He exists before everything, and in Him all holds together. He is the head of the body, His community. He is the beginning, the firstborn from the dead—so that He might come to have first place in all things. For God was pleased to have all His fullness dwell in Him.

To explain how God used a tallit of light to create all there is, some say He wrapped Himself in a prayer shawl and the light cast from that prayer shawl suffused all existence without beginning or end. Others say God took the light and stretched it like a garment, and the heavens continued to expand until God said enough, citing Job 37:3: "Under the whole heaven He lets it loose, and His light to the ends of the earth." I know many people who believe this, and I share it because I find it useful to consider when contemplating how God created the world. However, there is no factual evidence to support these views, and we can be certain only of the things Hashem has told us clearly in His Word.

Another legend related to the idea that God covers Himself in a tallit is the claim that God wore a fringed prayer shawl when He appeared to Moses on Mount Sinai so that Moses could comprehend God's instructions for creating the tallit by seeing a demonstration. The Bible does not explicitly say that God wore a tallit when He appeared to Moses, but we must ask another question: How would God have appeared to Moses? I believe He did so in the person of Yeshua preincarnate. Because I believe Yeshua obeyed the religious laws and always wore a tallit, He may in fact have appeared to Moses wearing a tallit. Therefore, when God revealed Himself to certain people through the person of Yeshua, He was probably wearing a tallit—but this is only speculation.

Some also believe God dons the tallit as we do so that He can pray parallel to our prayers. This may be true, but again we have no biblical evidence to support this claim. What we do know from Scripture is that Messiah is always making intercession for us, whether or not He does so while wearing a tallit. (See Romans 8:34 and Hebrews 7:25.)

YESHUA ENTERED JERUSALEM UNDER THE TALLIT

When Yeshua humbly rode into Jerusalem for the last time on the donkey, the people put their clothing or cloaks on the donkey, and others threw them on the road as He traveled. At this time they shouted, *"Baruch haba b'shem Adonai!"* (Blessed is He who comes in the name of the Lord!). Many believe the people were actually casting their tallitot from one side to the other so Yeshua would ride into Jerusalem under the tallit.

This makes sense because the tallitot would symbolize the anointing of Hashem upon Yeshua as He prepared for His final teaching in the temple, His last Passover, and His eventual crucifixion. But there does not seem to be any biblical or historical proof of this, so when I share this, I am always careful to note that this is not fact, but a possibility.

ELIJAH'S MANTLE (TALLIT) WAS PASSED TO JOHN

Elijah the prophet was supposedly a hairy man with a thunderous voice who wore a leather girdle and a tallit made out of camel's hair so it would not decay. Some believe the prophet passed on this priestly garment—which, of course, represented the name and Word of God—to the prophet Elisha, who received a double portion of the spirit that was upon Elijah. As the legend goes, there was no one to receive Elijah's mantle (tallit) after Elisha, so it was kept in the Holy Place at the Altar of Incense by the menorah until someone was found worthy to wear it.

When Zechariah was serving his time as *kohen* (priest) before Adonai, he was told by an angel of Adonai who appeared to him as he was standing at the right side of the Altar of Incense that his wife, Elizabeth, would give birth to a son and he was to be named John (Yochanan). Supposedly it was John (who became known as John the Immerser or John the Baptist) who was worthy of wearing the tallit of Elijah. Again, this story has not been proven, but it is certainly interesting!

YESHUA LEFT HIS TALLIT IN THE EMPTY TOMB

Another popular story about the tallit stems from the resurrection of the Messiah. We read in the Gospel of John:

> Early in the morning on the first day of the week, while it is still dark, Miriam from Magdala comes to the tomb. She sees that the stone had been rolled away from the tomb. So she comes running to Simon Peter and the other disciple, the one *Yeshua* loved. She tells them, "They've taken the Master out of the tomb, and we don't know where they've put Him!"
>
> Then Peter and the other disciple set out, going to the tomb. The two were running together, but the other disciple outran Peter and arrived at the tomb first. Leaning in, he sees the linen strips lying there. But he didn't go in.
>
> Then Simon Peter comes following him, and he entered the tomb. He looks upon the linen strips lying there, and the face cloth that had been on His head. It was not lying with the linen strips, but was rolled up in a place by itself. So then the

other disciple, who had reached the tomb first, also
entered. He saw and believed.

—John 20:1–8

According to ancient tradition, if you were invited
to dinner at someone's house and you enjoyed the meal
and the company, you would crumple up your napkin
and leave it on the table. However, if you didn't enjoy the
meal or the company, you would fold the linen napkin
and neatly place it on the table. That would be a sign that
you had a bad experience and would not be returning to
that place.

It is said that when the disciples arrived at the empty
tomb and saw the face cloth (tallit) folded and rolled up in
a place by itself, they understood that Yeshua was saying,
"I'm out of here and never coming back to this place." In
other words, "The Resurrection is complete. I have overcome death, received the victory for all creation, and will
never be doing this again!" Some claim this is why John
"saw and believed." Not only was Yeshua's body not there,
but He was risen and His mission was complete. This story
makes sense and may indeed be true. I include it here
because, again, it is not clear in Scripture that this is what
Messiah was intending to convey.

PAUL WAS A TALLIT MAKER

Because the word *tallit* can be defined in Aramaic as
"little tent," some have supposed that Rabbi Shaul (the
Apostle Paul) was a tallit maker, not a literal tent maker.
This is possible, but I have not found any definitive facts to

support this conclusion. Both a tallit and a tent are a type of cover, but that is the only relationship I have found that even remotely supports this claim.

THE TZITZIT EQUAL 613

The Hebrew numbers represent different values. Many rabbis say the tzitzit on the tallit represent the commandments because the Hebrew word for tzitzit (צִיצִת) has a numeric value of 613, and that is the number of the commandments. This seems to make sense, since the purpose of the tzitzit is to remind us to keep Hashem's commandments.

This is how they come to this calculation:

- Each *tzadhe* (צ) has a numerical value of ninety, and there are two, bringing the total to 180.

- Each *yod* (י) has a numerical value of ten, and there are two, bringing the total to twenty.

- The *tav* (ת) has a numerical value of four hundred.

Together this gives us six hundred. Then there are eight strings hanging down from the tzitzit and five knots. This makes thirteen, which when added to the previous six hundred brings our total to 613, which is the number of the commandments.[1]

Once again, this is more of a rabbinical calculation than a scriptural one. Whether there is an intentional correlation between the number of tzitzit and the number of commandments must be left to speculation. But what we do know is that the tallit reminds us to trust and honor God by being obedient to His Word!

THE TALLIT AS A CLOAK

Another common story about the tallit says it was used to identify those with a license to beg. In this passage from Mark 10, we read about Yeshua's interaction with a blind beggar named Bartimaeus.

> Then they came to Jericho. Now as *Yeshua* was leaving Jericho with His disciples and a large crowd, Bartimaeus the son of Timaeus, a blind beggar, was sitting by the roadside. When he heard that it was *Yeshua* of *Natzeret*, he began to cry out, "*Ben-David*, *Yeshua*! Have mercy on me!" Many were warning him to be quiet; but he kept crying out all the more, "*Ben-David*, have mercy on me!"
>
> *Yeshua* stopped and said, "Call him over."
>
> So they call the blind man, saying, "Take heart! Get up, He's calling you!" Throwing off his cloak, he jumped up and came to *Yeshua*.
>
> And answering him, *Yeshua* said, "What do you want Me to do for you?"
>
> The blind man said, "*Rabboni*, I want to see again!"
>
> *Yeshua* said to him, "Go! Your faith has made you well." Instantly he regained his sight and began following *Yeshua* down the road.
>
> —MARK 10:46–52

It is thought that in those days, a person who wished to derive public support from begging was required to go to the authorities in his region and present himself in person with documented proof of his disability or handicap. However, instead of being given a license in the form of a certificate, it was given in the form of a cloak of a certain color and style. Some claim the cloak Bartimaeus threw off when he heard the voice of Yeshua was "documentation" of his blindness. They say it showed great faith for him to throw it off before Yeshua touched him, and it was this act of faith that touched the heart of Messiah and led to the man's healing.

I do not have incontrovertible proof that beggars wore certain tallitot that served as documentation of their disability. But I do know this: Hashem responds to our faith. When we are willing to step out in faith and trust Yeshua's Word, we will see God's miracle-working power at work in our lives as well.

It is clear from the stories I have shared that many people recognize that the tallit is a special garment with spiritual significance for those who seek to understand it. But again we must remember, though the tallit is a sacred object, there is no power in the garment itself. The power lies in Hashem and in our choice to honor Him by obeying His Word, submitting to His covering and authority, and seeking Him in prayer. The tallit is not the Word or power of God, but it should be treated with honor and respect because it represents Hashem and His Word.

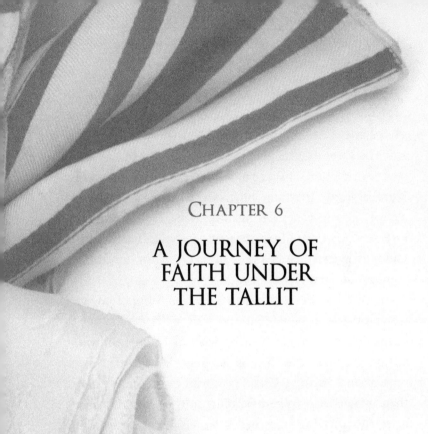

CHAPTER 6

A JOURNEY OF FAITH UNDER THE TALLIT

EVERYTHING ABOUT EXPERIENCING the mystery of the prayer shawl points to Yeshua, the Teacher. We come under the tallit of Yeshua through His blood and His love. The tallit is all about Him. It is the representation of the Word of God, and Yeshua is the living Word of God. The tallit reflects Hashem's presence, protection, power, covering, healing, hope, forgiveness, and love because the tallit represents Yeshua. Through faith and trust we receive His gifts of favor, mercy, forgiveness, compassion, and eternal love.

In this life we will have trials and tribulations, and we will battle to be patient and wait for God's answer to our problems. Though we may wish to avoid them, these struggles help our faith to grow. Faith is believing in the unseen and trusting God's promises even before we see them materialize. When we trust in the living God, miracles and amazing signs occur, which in turn help to further build our faith.

Faith has been a river running through my whole life, but it became a greater and more personal part of my life when I started my exciting journey with Yeshua. Even before I actually knew the Teacher, Hashem's hand was upon me. I can think back on many situations in which He was directing me either toward something or away from something. In the chaotic and politically tumultuous 1970s, I decided to travel with a friend of mine from Buffalo to California. It was just a few weeks before I would graduate from the State University of New York at Buffalo with my bachelor's degree in psychology.

During our trip we stopped in Ohio and visited Kent State and Ohio State. We were having fun, but at one point during the trip I felt that Hashem was telling me to return to Buffalo and get my degree, so I listened. As it turned out, the week my friend and I were there was just a few days before several students were killed in the infamous 1970 shooting at Kent State.

We all need the counsel of the Teacher—and He wants to direct us. Sometimes we listen and sometimes we don't. But whether or not we recognize His voice, He is always there!

Scripture tells us that "without faith it is impossible to please God. For the one who comes to God must believe that He exists and that *He is a rewarder of those who seek Him*" (Heb. 11:6, emphasis added). My mother-in-law is a perfect example of this. Iris was a Jewish woman who apparently had always believed in God but never really had any personal relationship with Him. In her later years she suffered from loneliness, the aches and pains that come along with aging, and the inevitable gradual decline of all the major systems of her body. Nevertheless, her mind remained sharp. She was a "take charge" person who always stated her opinion, whether you wanted to hear it or not, right up to the end of her life.

She came to many of our services and speaking engagements throughout her life and loved my "speeches," as she would call them. Unfortunately, for so many of her last years, she had a tremendous fear of dying, even to the point where she would sometimes not want to fall asleep because she was fearful of dying in her sleep. The blessing, however, came when she was ninety-eight years old and received Yeshua into her heart. All of a sudden she had a major personality change! She became more loving, thoughtful, and kind. Whenever she spoke to my wife and me, her words were always filled with love and she could not stop telling us how much she loved us. There had been a time when Racquel and her mother were not speaking at all, so this brought tremendous healing for my wife!

Despite my mother-in-law's newfound faith, she still feared dying. However, shortly after her amazing one hundredth birthday celebration, she found a delightful peace through her faith in Yeshua that enabled her to lie down without fear and look up into the spiritual realm, ready to leave for her eternal home. After a few days of this beautiful stillness, she traveled through the dimensions of eternal peace and bliss with the Creator. Iris has been rewarded because of her faith to see "the substance of things hoped for, the evidence of realities not seen" (Heb. 11:1).

WE ALL SERVE SOMEBODY

Faith is about light and darkness, good and evil. Bob Dylan said we all have to serve somebody, either the devil or the Lord. In almost every film that is made, there is a battle between good and evil or light and darkness. In older films clothing was evidence of what side a person was on: the good guys wore white and the bad guys wore black. God, however, is all light. Darkness is the absence of light. When God reigns in the Millennium, there will be no darkness. His presence will bring continuous light. There will be no need for light from the stars in the sky or the sun or moon because light will emanate from Him.

We must choose whom we will serve in this present life. Will we choose to live with Yeshua, or will we choose to reject the Teacher and live an eternity away from Him? As I stated previously, it all goes back to the Gan Eden when Adam and Eve were instructed to eat freely of any tree in the garden but to avoid the *Etz haDaat tov V'ra* (Tree of Knowledge of Good and Evil). Adam had to determine his priority: to obey Hashem or to obey his own temptations and desires. He chose the latter and tasted the fruit of his desire.

Yeshua is the one who brings unity to all things, resulting in the shining of His light. The spirit of the anti-Messiah has been trying to push mankind off God's track ever since the garden. All the adversity Abraham, Isaac, Jacob, Joseph, Saul, David, Solomon, and Israel encountered up to and including the death of Yeshua were attempts to defeat the purposes of God. But God has won the victory through Messiah!

Many of our human difficulties have doubt at their root. Doubt is a result of a lack of faith (*emunah*, אמונה) or trust (*bitachon*, בטחון). Without true faith or trust, we will never be able to decide which path to take in life. Deception, lies, depression, division, anger, bitterness, and frustration all come from the spirit of the anti-Messiah, whose purpose is to push us off the path to God and cause us to instead curse His name (*chillul Hashem*, which means "to desecrate the name of God").

Even when I did not yet know Yeshua, I had faith in Hashem, and many of my decisions were based upon that faith. It is not fear or adversity that causes us to take the wrong path; it is doubt or a lack of faith. Without doubt we could go through the fire if we knew we were following the path Hashem wanted us to take.

Yeshua said, "You shall know the truth, and the truth shall set you free" (John 8:32, MEV). But when we know only partial truth, we open ourselves—our heart, mind, and spirit—to doubt and deception.

The adversary of God uses doubt to lead us to deception. If the forbidden tree had just been the Tree of Knowledge of Evil, Adam and Eve might have made the correct choice because people want to avoid evil. However, it was the Tree of the Knowledge of Good and Evil that was forbidden. The adversary deceived Adam and Eve into questioning whether they really had knowledge of all that was good, and that led them to doubt God's Word.

Sin then caused them to hide from God. How could they hide from someone whose presence is everywhere? Doubt leads to deceptive thinking, and deceptive thinking leads us to make the wrong decisions! For instance, we may have faith that God exists, but we may not trust Him enough to surrender to His sovereign control. Because we are not fixing our eyes on Him as the author and finisher of our faith (Heb. 12:2), the truth becomes blurred, and we try to solve problems on our own.

The tallit reminds us of God's Word, and Yeshua is the Living Word. As we discover the mysteries of the prayer shawl, we must remember to always walk in faith in Yeshua, not in doubt or fear. Hashem will bring goodness and beauty from all of our trials and tears. His Word says so. It tells us He will give "beauty for ashes, the oil of joy for mourning, the garment of praise for the spirit of heaviness, that they might be called oaks of righteousness, the planting of ADONAI, that He may be glorified" (Isa. 61:3).

Entering Hashem's presence by wearing the tallit causes

us to come into the secret place with Yeshua. This in turn builds up our faith and turns our doubt into trust. When we embark on our journey of faith, searching for the everlasting, always-existing Light, we must realize that the beginning of the path is always surrounded by darkness. Darkness is the absence of light, and humankind removed itself from the Light back in the Gan Eden. Yeshua is the Light, and Adonai has promised to give us "treasures of darkness and hidden riches of secret places, so [we] may know that [He is] ADONAI, the God of Israel, who calls [us] by [our] name" (Isa. 45:3).

This walk of faith has its trials and tribulations. Sometimes there is so much darkness that we really can't see what is in front of us. However, in faith we take the steps ahead and move forward. When my wife and I received His calling to move from Palm Beach Gardens to Orlando, Florida, it didn't make sense to us, but in faith we prepared and took the steps to move forward on the Teacher's path for us. Darkness was before us, and we gave up a lot because our family was mostly in South Florida. The chess pieces on Yeshua's master chessboard were rearranged, but we found many of His "treasures of darkness" as we walked onward in faith.

The Almighty humbled Himself to live with us as a human being and travel through darkness, poverty, and constant trials—from infancy, filth, and rejection to a horrific death on a tree (cross)—just so He could identify with us and enable His light, which existed before creation, to be our light too. As we identify with Him, we pass from darkness to light and He permits us to experience His presence and glimpse His *kavod*, His glory. In that secret place, with our heads covered by the tallit, we do experience His kavod!

A LIFESTYLE OF FAITH

Once Racquel and I were speaking in Atlanta and had a week of potent ministry through the fire and power of the Ruach HaKodesh. As we were driving back to the home of the gracious people who invited us, we were on a very busy highway. There was a tremendous amount of traffic, and it was raining very hard. I was driving in the middle lane and decided to get into the right lane so I could go slower. As I glanced in my rearview mirror, I noticed that the car behind me looked like it was skidding and coming right toward me. I turned on my signal to indicate that I would be moving into the right lane, but then I skidded and there was no place for me to turn.

I am certain there was no open space for me to direct my car into the right lane. However, Yeshua appeared to push the car ahead of me forward and slow up the car behind me and place my car right where it belonged between the two cars in the right lane. Our adrenaline was flowing, but we just gave thanks to Yeshua. We could have said we were "lucky," or we could have given thanks to the One who protected us. We did the latter.

Faith is a way of life. It is a path that we choose to take. It is a belief that there is no such thing as a coincidence. A person of faith believes that each happening is a "God-incidence." In the previous example, were we lucky, or did God orchestrate our safety? Faith is knowing that Hashem is with us wherever we go and giving Him the glory and thanks for all things. Many times when we face problems, we attribute our struggles to Hashem. This is because we have set up idols of stone within our hearts. These idols are our pride and intellect. Hashem told His people, "Nor are you to set up a pillar for yourself—*ADONAI* your God hates this" (Deut. 16:22). God hated stone pillars because they represented man's idols, those things they trusted in more than Him. We must get rid of the idols in our hearts and allow Yeshua to guide us.

When we walk by faith, we walk in God's kingdom authority, which allows us to see His power demonstrated in our lives and His name glorified in the earth. Many times faith in Hashem and His Word will cause us to be mocked, scorned, and perceived as naïve. Whenever we face derision for our walk of faith, we must remember to always reflect Yeshua in our response. He is the Shepherd (John 10:11), and we are the sheep of His pasture (Ps. 100:3). We must follow His example.

Though we may face scorn for following Yeshua, taking the journey of faith is not a sign of weakness. It is an expedition of commitment, submission, obedience, and sacrifice. We are made up of body, soul (mind and emotions), and spirit. When we choose the path of faith and trust, our spirit, which is connected to His Spirit, reigns over our mind and emotions, and we are able to produce lasting fruit for God's kingdom!

Racquel and I have had our faith tested over and over again in our thirty years of serving Yeshua. There have been times when we felt like giving up, but instead of surrendering to the adversary of Hashem, we continued to have faith in Yeshua. We stood on His Word, believing what He said is true, and we began to see the glory of God (John 11:40). Miracles occurred in our lives because we believed in Yeshua. It was as Adonai said to Moses, "Is ADONAI's arm too short? Now you will see whether My word will come true for you or not" (Num. 11:23). Again and again we have seen His word come true for us!

Yeshua wants to work miracles in all of our lives. In most cases it is our doubt or unbelief that blocks Him from accomplishing His perfect will in us. Because of our faith, close to thirty years ago my wife and I experienced a crisis in our family. Despite the devastation it brought to our hearts and spirits, the very night we were going through our own personal trial, we were asked to go to the hospital to visit a man we didn't know. His family requested us because the man was on his deathbed and did not know the Teacher. Our hearts were heavy with our own pain, but we knew this was a matter of eternal life or death, so we traveled to the hospital and introduced the man to Yeshua, whom he proceeded to ask into his heart.

When you live a life of faith, you will find it necessary to "contend for the faith" (Jude 3). That is what we had to do when our family was in crisis. During that season my wife in particular had an emotional hole in her heart that would not heal. We prayed for the situation to change. We fasted, cried, and begged Adonai, but nothing seemed to change. One day my wife told Hashem that if the situation never improved, she would still love and serve Him. Three days later God answered our prayers for our family! The reconciliation we were seeking took place more than ten years ago, and those relationships are now tremendously blessed and get stronger each day.

We must actively have faith in God's Word to see miracles occur. My wife and I have learned that we must put our faith to work for His glory. Just as the man with the withered hand stretched out his hand to receive healing, we must actively believe God to experience His glorious victories in our lives! (See Matthew 12:9–14.)

Our faith in Yeshua will be tested. But every life challenge is an opportunity to grow with the Teacher and become more like Him. The quality of our lives is not dependent on external situations. It is not dependent on how smooth or chaotic our lives are. It is dependent on how we conduct ourselves when we face frustrations and trials in life. Each test is to perfect our character. This truth plays out in a wonderful, heart-wrenching movie called *Ushpizin* (The Guests), which we view each Sukkot (Feast of Tabernacles). In the film, Moshe and Mali Bellanga are an impoverished couple who long for a child. Moshe seems to face trial after trial. When he is passed over for a bonus he expected, they cannot pay their bills and they certainly cannot prepare for Sukkot.

Moshe covers his head with his tallit and cries out to God for help. Afterward they receive a surprise financial gift right before Sukkot, allowing them to prepare for the holiday. But then they receive unexpected guests from Moshe's past who create many new challenges for Moshe and his wife. Yet ultimately he passes the test of faith through endurance, and in time he receives Hashem's most glorious blessing—a beautiful son.[1]

In each difficult situation ask yourself, "How can I allow what happened to transform me so I become more like Hashem?" When his faith was challenged, Moshe

Bellanga covered his head with his tallit and cried out to Hashem. When situations appear hopeless, put on your tallit, look at the tzitzit, and know that God is with you and His Word never changes. Receive His promised love. With Him, there is no hopelessness.

The situation must have looked bleak for the *talmidim*, the disciples of Yeshua. They hoped and believed that Yeshua was the Messiah, the Redeemer of Israel. However, He had been crucified and was dead and buried. It was now the third day after it all happened. This could have been the fatal blow to their faith. With disappointment heavy in their hearts, they prepared to leave Jerusalem. But then the Messiah appeared to them. In fact, in Luke 24:13–31, He walked with some of the disciples and they didn't even realize it!

Can you identify? Have you ever hoped and believed that God was going to redeem a situation in your life and found yourself losing heart while waiting for the answer you sought? What do we do when we have been waiting, praying, and believing, yet everything appears to be falling apart? We must realize that Yeshua is still with us. He walks with us and talks to us. He brings us hope through our faith. When pandemonium comes into our lives, we must "contend for the faith" (Jude 3). Remaining steadfast in our faith in Yeshua brings us peace. Whenever we call upon Him, He is near, always desiring to give us His shalom—His perfect peace.

In an instant Yeshua can send forth His word and a great light will shine forth, causing all darkness to disappear. Whenever you feel despair, it is because you believe that all is hopeless. Hopelessness is darkness—when you think God is absent. But when you come under the tallit and call upon Yeshua in faith, He can instantaneously shine His light into your situation and bring healing.

TRUST IN YESHUA

Trust (bitachon) is the awareness that the God in whom you believe is omnipresent, omniscient, and omnipotent. He is the Creator and in control of all things.

Our youngest daughter's wedding was a time of much-needed faith. It was the most magnificent wedding that I had ever attended. Everything was first-class and beautiful. However, when you are part of something so outstanding in the physical realm, you must be on guard for the probable warfare in the spiritual realm. It is in times like these that your faith must be strong!

First, I was the officiating rabbi at the wedding, and as I was preparing my thoughts, my computer decided not to work. Unfortunately I am used to that occurring at crucial times, so I was able to pray and get through it. Then on the Friday night before the wedding, I had a dream in which I was trying to go somewhere. The dream caused me to get out of bed, and when I did, I tripped on the sheet, fell, and knocked my head on the corner of the night table in our hotel room. Since I was bleeding, I had to call downstairs for some first aid. Fortunately, by the time of the wedding, I was fine. I covered the scar with some of my wife's makeup, and no one knew the difference.

Unfortunately that wasn't the last of the obstacles. On the day of the wedding, I had to run over to the country club to check on something for the ceremony. As I was returning to the hotel, I saw the car in front of me run a red light and crash into another car. Needless to say, my adrenaline was working overtime! Glass shattered and the cars were dented, but everyone seemed to be fine. That morning I took a long prayer walk like I usually did and covered everyone in the wedding party and those coming to the wedding in prayer. In faith I believed that everything would turn out superbly, and it did.

Faith in God is knowing that He exists, while trust is knowing that He is in control of your life. Trust in God is a must to help combat spiritual warfare. We can't pretend that spiritual warfare doesn't exist. It does, and we have the victory through our trust in Him and by using the weapons of warfare He has given us! (See 2 Corinthians 10:3–6 and Ephesians 6:11–18.)

Prayer leader Rebecca Greenwood wrote that "even when we do not know and see all the things that have been promised to us—when we have prayed for years for a specific breakthrough and it has not yet come, when circumstances in our lives are going the exact opposite direction they should be, when people let us down or betray us, when we are being pressed through financially difficult times—we can put our hope and trust in the Lord and expect that He is going to prove Himself faithful on our behalf."[2] We can strengthen our trust in El Shaddai every time we wrap ourselves in the tallit and see the tzitzit and remember God's Word. Just as we must be faithful to obey what Hashem has commanded us, so is He faithful to do what He promised. He will provide for us, He will protect us, and He will never leave us.

In the Torah, Adonai spoke to Moses, instructing him

to send out men to investigate the land that He was giving to Israel. The people of Israel knew that God existed, and they had seen the miracles that brought their freedom from Egyptian slavery. He also gave them food and water every day, and their clothes did not wear out! However, when the twelve scouts, each representing a tribe of Israel, were exploring the Promised Land, ten brought back a bad report. Only two of them, Joshua and Caleb, brought back a good report. The ten saw all the obstacles and became fearful and intimidated, but two had a different spirit. They saw the obstacles as a way for Adonai to show His power and glory. They had a spirit of bitachon, or trust, in the Word of Adonai.

Trusting Hashem in our everyday lives is knowing that He is on the throne and will never leave us or forsake us. The Lord kept His promise and brought the children of Israel into the Promised Land, but He punished the unbelieving generation by consigning them to wander in the wilderness for forty years until they had died off.

> ADONAI answered, "I have forgiven them just as you have spoken. But as certainly as I live and as certainly as the glory of ADONAI fills the entire earth, none of the people who saw My glory and My miraculous signs I performed in Egypt and in the wilderness—yet tested Me these ten times and did not obey My Voice—not one of them will see the land I promised to their forefathers. None of those who treated Me with contempt will see it! However, My servant Caleb, because a different spirit is with him and he is wholeheartedly behind Me, I will

bring him into the land where he went—his off-
spring will inherit it."

—NUMBERS 14:20–24

The only members of that generation who entered the
land of promise were Joshua, who succeeded Moses, and
Caleb, who had "a different spirit." God brought them into
the Promised Land because of their trust in Him.

When we trust in Yeshua, it means that we draw our
assurance from God, and with it we receive His shalom
and freedom from any anxiety or anger. We have two
paths from which to choose. We can choose the path of
doubt and unbelief, or we can fix our eyes on Adonai in
His holy temple (Ps. 11) and live in His presence and power.
Yeshua said, "Do not worry about tomorrow, for tomorrow
will worry about itself. Each day has enough trouble of its
own" (Matt. 6:34).

Come into His presence under the tallit. He will do
exceedingly abundantly more than we can ask or imagine
by His power that is at work in us (Eph. 3:20). Trust Him.
Conquer unbelief. Recognize and repent of any sin in your
life so nothing hinders your communication with Him.
You can be set free from any anger, bitterness, resentment,
rage, fear, and the like, for "in Him we live and move and
have our being" (Acts 17:28, MEV). Trust Him!

Anxiety and anger rent free space in our minds. They
keep us from using the gifts Yeshua has given us to employ
for His glory because we allow ourselves to focus on our
needs and problems instead of on His will and love for us.
Trust, however, leaves a person free to serve Yeshua with
all his heart, soul, spirit, and strength. When we can serve

Him unhindered, we are more likely to be fruitful in our walk with Him because we are able to hear His voice and thus obey His divine will.

What spirit is operating in you? Do you choose faith and trust, or fear and anxiety? We should all strive to be like Caleb and have a "different spirit" and be "whole-heartedly behind" Hashem. Being a person of faith will make a profound difference in the quality of your life!

BELIEVE YESHUA'S WORD

Wearing the tallit is a sign that you believe the Word of Adonai. It symbolizes the Teacher spreading over you His tzitzit or kanaph or the corner of His garment. It represents the Word of Adonai. When we wear the tallit for a certain function, we indicate our trust in the truth and power of God's Word. We are demonstrating our faith!

Adonai gave a message to the prophet Ezekiel telling him to "confront Jerusalem with her abominations" (Ezek. 16:2). God said:

> "Again I passed by and saw you, and behold, you
> were truly at the time of love. I spread the corner of
> my garment over you and covered your nakedness. I
> swore to you and entered into a covenant with you,"
> says *ADONAI*. "So you became Mine."
>
> —Ezekiel 16:8

Hashem gave this message to Israel because He wanted the people to remember from where they came. He was using Ezekiel to rebuke Israel for being rebellious and to remind them that they belong to Him. He had spread the corner of His garment, His spiritual tallit, over Israel. If they would only walk by faith and not by the evil desires of their hearts, they would experience His blessing!

In the last days, as darkness continues to spread over the nations, people will come from around the world to Jerusalem to seek the favor of Adonai:

> Thus says *ADONAI-Tzva'ot* [LORD of Hosts], "In those days it will come to pass that ten men from every language of the nations will grasp the corner of the garment of a Jew saying, 'Let us go with you, for we have heard that God is with you.'"
> —ZECHARIAH 8:23

Why would these people want to grasp the tzitzit of every Jew? It is because the tallit represents the Word of God, and there will be a great revival in which the Jewish people and then the nations will once again have their spiritual eyes, ears, and hearts open to comprehend the richness of His Word—the Torah, the Prophets, the Writings, and the New Covenant—and receive the Teacher into their hearts.

When I was taking physical therapy for the plantar fasciitis in my foot, I asked about a certain type of tape that I had heard would promote healing when put on the affected area. The therapist responded by telling me that there is a tape that you can put on your back in order to keep your posture in the correct position. When your back is in proper alignment, your gait is corrected, thus helping any back, knee, or foot problems to start to heal. This reminded me of the purpose of the tallit, or the Word of Adonai. The Word is to be our guide and our tutor to keep us on Hashem's path. When we diverge from the path, the Ruach HaKodesh will act like that special tape and nudge us back into alignment, if we are willing to listen and obey.

Yeshua said, "For to the one who has, more shall be given, and he shall have an abundance. But from the one who does not have, even what he does have shall be taken away" (Matt. 25:29). The one who listens to the Word of Adonai has spiritual wisdom because he receives it through faith, which comes by hearing the Word of Messiah. But the one who does not listen will not receive spiritual wisdom, and what spiritual wisdom he has will be taken away. Consequently, we can understand why the people of the nations will want to grab the hem of the garment (tzitzit) of the Jew in the last days. Those who desire to grab the tzitzit of the tallit will be the ones who listen and gain spiritual wisdom from Yeshua, and as His Word says in Matthew 25, they will receive an abundance!

EXPECT GOD TO ANSWER

Hashem wants us to overflow with hope by the power of the Ruach HaKodesh. It is this hope that gives us a tremendous expectancy of greater things to come. We must return to the resilient and convincing hope the fathers of our faith had from Abraham forward. The whole world today is desperately looking for hope and in need of strong, robust faith. Yeshua is the Master of hope.

Are you allowing fear or insecurity to keep you from doing what God is calling you to do? We must stay on course. We must keep and strengthen our faith in Him. We must not let trials and tribulations change our direction. We know that trials will come, but "happy is the one who endures testing, because when he has stood the test, he will receive the crown of life, which the Lord promised to those who love Him" (Jacob [James] 1:12). We must continue to "contend for the faith." We must strengthen ourselves and build up our most holy faith by praying in the Ruach HaKodesh.

For many months my wife and I had been praying for the baby who would be in our youngest daughter's womb. Daily when we would pray for our daughter and son-in-law, we would also include the baby. We were praying with expectancy. Then one day as I prayed, Yeshua told me to pray for the baby that *is* in her womb. When I told Racquel, we both believed that she was pregnant, and we found out a few weeks later that indeed she was!

We must pray fervently, and with expectation we must grab the hem of Yeshua's tallit. That is the great hope Yeshua has given to us—that when we faithfully seek Him, He will answer.

CHAPTER 7

THE TALLIT
AS A BRIDGE

A FEW YEARS AGO the congregation I lead, Congregation Gesher Shalom, hosted a Night to Honor Israel event at a large Baptist church in our city. Close to two thousand people attended, and our facility could not have accommodated a crowd that large. For this reason we asked the pastor of the Baptist church, who is a friend, if we could use his sanctuary for the gathering. He graciously allowed us to do so, and as a thank-you our synagogue presented to him a beautiful tallit and prayed for him as I wrapped him in this new tallit. As he graciously received the gift, he commented, "This is the most Jewish thing to do."

Indeed, a tallit is often given as a way of blessing a person and showing your heart. But by presenting this pastor with a tallit, I was also acknowledging that we are brothers in Yeshua and united in His love.

For almost fifteen years the Messianic Jewish Alliance of America (MJAA) has invited a Christian speaker to participate in one of the seven nightly plenary sessions of our international Messiah Conference, which is held annually in Grantham, Pennsylvania. Each year we present a tallit as a gift of thanks and pray for the speaker. It is a time of blessing and anointing. And yes, presenting a tallit is the most Jewish thing for us to do!

One very well-known pastor, a man with a huge international ministry, was so thankful when we presented a tallit to him that he told me he considered me his rabbi. He said any time he comes into my area to speak, I have an open invitation to attend the meeting, and if I show up, he will have a seat for me right up front.

Why am I sharing these accounts? Because they remind

us that the tallit is one of Yeshua's treasures that can connect us with other networks in the spiritual realm. Ever since the Gan Eden there has been separation and division: man from God, man from man, man from woman, the land of Israel from the nation of Israel, the people of Israel from Yeshua. In the body of Messiah, there has been division due to prejudices of color, background, how to use the gifts of the Spirit, class, cultural background, and theology. Yet when two parties who have been in direct opposition for thousands of years stand together under the tallit of God, it represents a *gesher shalom*, a bridge (גשר) of peace (שלום), which could only come through the work of Messiah.

This is what happens every Shabbat at the congregation I lead. When we—both those born Jewish and those not born Jewish—stand under the tallit for the Aaronic Benediction (from Numbers 6:24–26, which begins: "The LORD bless you and keep you..."), we see a *selah*, or a pause in time. All divisions come to a halt. The Word of God covers us as we stand together under the banner of Yeshua, the Messiah. There is no separation because, for those few sanctified seconds, Hashem's children—of different genders, colors, classes, cultures, and philosophies, all surrendered to the same God—are standing in one accord, of one mind and heart, as one new man.

This is the heart of Yeshua—that we would be echad (one) as He is echad. In the last few years there has been a resurgence of division and hatred between diverse groups of people. The news reports are filled with killing and attempted murder, all types of violence and sexual assault, political division, anger, bitterness, and disgust. Once again anti-Semitism is rearing its ugly head, and there is a horrific and demonic torturing of people who profess faith in Adonai. There are nonsensical battles over "political correctness" of all stripes. This is a reality that could be transformed so simply.

If each of us could just surrender our all to the true Father of all creation by coming under the tallit of the Teacher, a miraculous change would occur. Because of mankind's sin Adonai wiped out a generation through a flood, but He covenanted to never do that again. Since that time He has sent His Messiah, Yeshua, to shed His blood on the altar of the heavenly tabernacle for the justification of our sins so we may all enter under His tallit of love.

The tallit symbolizes a bridge that unifies. Yeshua covers whoever chooses to come under His tallit, His chuppah, and receive Him as Savior. In Yeshua we see all different types of people becoming echad as He and the Father are echad. His banner over us is love (Song of Sol. 2:4)! It sounds so elementary, but that's the amazing mystery that those who came before us always desired to solve. If we would truly surrender to Yeshua and allow Him to renew our minds and receive His Spirit, we would experience this amazing oneness in Him and He could use us as His vessels to fulfill His purposes.

THE TALLIT OF YACHAD (UNITY) AT MOUNT SINAI

Imagine that on a wall you see a beautiful painting of Mount Sinai with light shining from it. As you walk closer to it, you see that Mount Sinai is made up of the five books of Moses, with the name of each book written in Hebrew. You also see five people who appear to be at the base of the mountain. Each is covering his head with a tallit, and their faces are all turned toward the mountain. When you look even closer, you realize that between those five people and the base of the mountain are millions of people, with each person wearing his own tallit. The light appears to be a divine radiance that emanates from the center of the mountaintop to the ends of it, and the people seem to be covered by the light. Thick clouds of glory, which represent the presence of Adonai, are above the mountain.

A very special friend of ours gave Racquel and me this painting from Israel as a gift in the mid-1990s. It is absolutely magnificent, and we have it hanging prominently on a wall in our home. It inspired me to think of the tallit as a bridge because the "multitudes" of people standing at the base of Mount Sinai consisted of God's Jewish people and those from other nations who believed in the God of Abraham, Isaac, and Jacob after seeing the power He displayed when He delivered His people from Egypt. From the beginning it was the plan of Shaddai to bring Israel and the nations together in unity. The divine light in that painting symbolizes to me the tallit of Yeshua covering all His people as one family together in His presence!

This gathering at Mount Sinai took place on the first Shavuot (Feast of Weeks), the third month after the Jewish people were delivered from Egypt. Israel had set up camp in the wilderness right in front of the base of the mountain:

> Moses went up to God, and ADONAI called to him
> from the mountain saying, "Say this to the house

of Jacob, and tell *Bnei-Yisrael*, 'You have seen what I did to the Egyptians, and how I carried you on eagle's wings and brought you to Myself. Now then, if you listen closely to My voice, and keep My covenant, then you will be My own treasure from among all people, for all the earth is Mine. So as for you, you will be to Me a kingdom of *kohanim* and a holy nation'"...All the people answered together and said, "Everything that ADONAI has spoken, we will do." Then Moses reported the words of the people to ADONAI.

—EXODUS 19:3–6, 8

All the people answered in unity and were in one accord. They responded by saying that they would "do and obey" (*na'aseh v'nishma*) all that Adonai had said. Can you imagine three million Jewish people and the multitudes in total agreement? There was thunder, lightning, smoke, fire, and long blasts of the shofar at the revelation at Sinai.

THE TALLIT OF YACHAD IN JERUSALEM

Fifteen hundred years later, again on Shavuot (the Festival of Weeks), a similar event occurred at the temple in Jerusalem (Acts 2). Ten days before the talmidim (disciples) went to Jerusalem, they were praying and were in unity. On Shavuot they were still in unity, or "with one mind" (Acts 2:46), just like the multitude at Sinai fifteen hundred years earlier. Pious men from all the nations again were gathered together, and Adonai through the Ruach HaKodesh was intensely present. The sound of a powerful rushing wind filled the room, and tongues like fire fell upon them.

Then thousands of the Jewish people repented of their sins and dedicated themselves to Yeshua's instructions, which they heard through the *shlichim* (apostles), and to breaking bread and prayer. They became part of the Messianic community and were in one accord, having everything in common. Every day they spent time together at the temple and went house to house worshipping, praying, praising God, and fellowshipping together. Once again, Jewish men and women and those from other nations were all in one accord.

When there is unity, the power and fire of Shaddai can fall in a most impressive and effective way. One of the problems we have in the political realm today is that most of the politicians cannot come into agreement, and as a result the important issues do not get addressed. To paraphrase the Teacher, a people divided will fall (Mark 3:24–25). Yeshua wants us to be like those at the base of Mount Sinai and especially like those in the temple in Jerusalem. He wants us to surrender to Him our prideful ways so that we may be echad as He is echad.

Humility brings unity. When we humble ourselves before one another and Adonai, we experience favor (*chen*) in the eyes of God and in the eyes of other believers. We then begin to love one another as the Teacher would have us to. This resulting unity would be tremendously powerful. When this occurs, miracles, signs, and wonders are prevalent, and the fire and power of God are so evident that all the glory, praise, and honor could only go to Him!

THE GESHER (BRIDGE)

In 1995 this inspiration about *yachad* (unity) caused my wife and me to begin our ministry, Gesher International. As the Scriptures say, "*Hinei ma tov umanaim shevet achim gam yachad*," which is translated, "Behold, how good and pleasant it is for brothers to dwell together in unity!" (Ps. 133:1). Our purpose was to build bridges in the body of Messiah by leading a ministry of reconciliation, as the Scriptures describe: "Now all these things are from God, who reconciled us to Himself through Messiah and gave us the ministry of reconciliation" (2 Cor. 5:18).

In the Bible unity is compared to the precious oil that begins on the head and flows down through the beard. The two stick together and become very difficult to separate. Unity is also compared to the dew that falls on the grass. Hashem is making the point that unity is something to be grasped, and once we are united, we should not be separated. The dew falling on grass also suggests that unity helps us grow. As brothers and sisters we need to work out our differences and humbly surrender to Adonai. Unity is His desire for us, and any desire of His should be our utmost priority.

The eighteenth century Hasidic leader Rabbi Nachman of Bratslav said, "The whole world is a very narrow bridge; the important thing is not to be afraid."[1] The mission of Gesher International is to bridge hearts through the ministry of reconciliation. By building relationships and through education we can narrow our differences and expand our similarities. As we bridge hearts, trust and love will replace fear. Then we can draw closer to the heart of Messiah so we can be echad, as epitomized by Yeshua and the Father.

The purpose of a bridge (gesher) is to bring two parts together and make them one (unity). For example, the bridge on a pair of eyeglass frames brings the two lenses and ear pieces together in unity so they can function as one piece and create single, simultaneous binocular vision. When we recite the Shema, we are saying, "*Shema Yisrael* ADONAI *Eloheinu* ADONAI *Echad*" (Hear, O Israel, the LORD is our God, the LORD is One). If Adonai is telling Israel that He is echad, the unity or composite of one, then He certainly wants all of His people to be one. His purpose has always been to bring us together with one mind, not in uniformity but in unity.

A BRIDGE FOR ISRAEL

It has always been Hashem's purpose that Israel would stand united with one mind and one heart. That happened when in one day Israel reemerged as a nation on its God-given land, as Scripture foretold:

> Before she was in labor, she gave birth. Before her pain came, she delivered a male child. Who has heard such a thing? Who has seen such things? Can a land be born in one day? Can a nation be brought forth at once? For as soon as Zion was in labor, she gave birth to her children. "Will I bring the moment of birth, and not give delivery?" says ADONAI. "Will I who cause delivery shut up the womb?" says your God. Rejoice with Jerusalem, and be glad with her,

all you who love her. Rejoice for joy with her all you
who mourned over her.

—ISAIAH 66:7–10

Israel was brought together on the land, but unfortunately our sinful souls, minds, and emotions have kept us apart since then. Jerusalem has and always will be the capital of Israel, but many want to divide up the land. All who fight against Israel's right to possess its land are fighting against the God of Israel. Those who are boycotting, divesting from, and putting sanctions on Israel are doing this to the God of Israel. It doesn't matter the church, synagogue, or denomination to which you belong. It doesn't matter what your intellectual or political opinions are telling you. What matters is how obedient you are to the Word of God.

Adam and Eve made the same error, and it has affected humankind for nearly six thousand years! *Did God really say that?* This is the same question the adversary asked back in the garden. Remember, "There is nothing new under the sun" (Eccles. 1:9)!

Do you really think you can win a battle against Hashem? His Word never changes. It is the same yesterday, today, and forever! When you fight against Israel, you are fighting against His Word; when you fight against His Word, you are eating the fruit of the Tree of Knowledge of Good and Evil and consequently fighting against Him! Hashem said, "My desire is to bless those who bless you, but whoever curses you I will curse, and in you all the families of the earth will be blessed" (Gen. 12:3).

It is no accident that the tallit is reflected in the flag of

Israel. It has a blue Star of David on a white background between two blue stripes. The color blue reminds us of the color dye traditionally used for the tekhelet. As I again think about the painting of Mount Sinai, with its image of divine light, the clouds of glory, and the fire by night shining upon the Israelites along with the people bridged together under His wings (His tallit), both Israelites and "resident outsiders," I can imagine the flag of Israel waving proudly over all those standing there in one mind and heart. How glorious that would be! That kind of unity is possible because Yeshua has already defeated the adversary in the spiritual realm and has become the bridge that will cause Israel and the nations to enter into the chuppah, the tallit of Yeshua HaMashiach (the Messiah), together as His bride.

HASHEM'S PLAN FOR UNITY

> Then God said, "Let Us make man in Our image, after Our likeness!"…God created humankind in His image, in the image of God He created him, male and female He created them."
>
> —GENESIS 1:26–27

When God created man and put Adam in is His perfect paradise, it was His desire that humankind would be a type of Israel, a civilization that prevails with Him. His heart was that we would be in unity with one another and with Yeshua, that we would be one with Him and the Father. In Scripture a man was to leave his father and mother and cling to his wife (Gen. 2:24). They were to be one with each other and one with Yeshua. Nonetheless, when the woman, Eve (Chava), fell into deception and broke God's commandment and Adam followed suit, there began a separation in creation that has existed throughout history.

The power of the Teacher's victory over the adversary has brought Yeshua's balm of healing over all separation or division in the spiritual realm, but it is still being worked out in the physical realm. This physical separation will be totally healed when we begin to dwell with Yeshua in the Millennium. On the seventh day of the last thousand years (the Shabbat), we will rest in Yeshua, and He will rest in His creation, as He did on the seventh day of creation.

From the point when sin separated mankind from God in the garden onward, a bridge was needed to restore the unity that existed in paradise. There was now a separation even between the Tree of Life and the Tree of the Knowledge of Good and Evil. Humankind could not be trusted, so we were expelled from the Gan Eden, and Adonai Elohim placed *cheruvim* at the entrance to the garden to guard the way to the Tree of Life with flaming swords.

Cain's sin in killing his brother Abel was a result of the separation that existed in the spiritual realm and manifested in the physical realm. Sin and evil were rampant in society in Cain's day. But Hashem had a plan. Adam and Eve were intimate and had another son they named Seth. To Seth also a son was born, who was named Enosh. At that time, some of the people began to pray and call out to God.

In the ten generations from Adam to Noah, the wickedness of man had become great on the earth, with every intent of the thoughts of the heart being continually only evil (Gen. 6:5). This evil inclination (yetzer hara) was a result of the separation from Adonai that took place in the garden. The evil only grew worse and worse until finally in Noah's generation Hashem decided to wipe out humankind because He regretted making them. But Noah found favor in Adonai's eyes and was considered blameless among his generation (Gen. 6:6–9).

It may seem as if the yetzer hara took Hashem by surprise. However, when you take the Hebrew meanings of the names of the sons born from Adam to Noah, you read a message from Hashem: "Man is appointed mortal sorrow, but the blessed God shall come down teaching that His death will bring the despairing comfort [or rest]."[2]

HEBREW	ENGLISH
ADAM	MAN
SETH	APPOINTED
ENOSH	MORTAL
KENAN	SORROW
MAHALALEL	THE BLESSED GOD
JARED	SHALL COME DOWN
ENOCH	TEACHING
METHUSELAH	HIS DEATH SHALL BRING
LAMECH	THE DESPAIRING
NOAH	REST, OR COMFORT

Shaddai had it figured out all along! Even before Creation, the bridge leading to the eternal garden of God was Yeshua. From the beginning Hashem had a plan to restore the unity between God and His people.

But the unity Hashem seeks is a unity under His banner, not one we manufacture. You may recall that humankind came together as one in ancient Babylon in the land of Shinar. They spoke the same language, but that prideful spirit of Lucifer rose again, and the people of the earth sought to build a tower up to the heavens so they could be like God.

When Yeshua decided to come down and see what they were doing, He confused their language and spread them over the entire land. This is why their building project was called the Tower of Babel. (See Genesis 11:1–9.)

The problem with mankind coming together as they did in ancient Babylon is that, unless our sinful nature is drastically changed and we have unity under the tallit of Messiah, we will repeat the same prideful behavior and continue to miss the mark. The only way we can connect with the Father is through the bridge to Him—Yeshua.

After the incident with the Tower of Babel in the land of Shinar, Hashem's plan was to bring the whole world together—but in His way, not man's way. He called Abraham out from the land of Ur of the Chaldeans, telling him to leave his family and go to where He would send him. This is referred to as *Lech-Lecha*, which means "go" or "leave." Hashem made a covenant with Abraham that He would make his name great; and whoever would bless him and his seed would be blessed, and whoever would curse him and his seed would be cursed; and that through him all the nations of the world would be blessed (Gen. 12:1–3). Abraham would be called a Hebrew (*Ivrit*), which means "boundary crosser."

We can see that from the beginning it was God's plan

to make a family of the Hebrew people and the nations. Nevertheless, the separation that began in the garden continued. From Abraham's seed, there was division between his sons, Isaac and Ishmael; and his grandsons, Jacob and Esau; and finally his great-grandsons, Joseph and his brothers. Yet Hashem's covenant with Abraham continued throughout the generations and is still in effect today.

Abraham's seed was together and in one accord at the revelation of Sinai, and together they said they would do and obey (na'aseh v'nishma) all that God had spoken (Exod. 19:8). The next forty-two generations were met with trials and tribulations, the ecstasy of victory and the agony of defeat, the gain and loss of power, the rise and fall of kings from the line of Judah; but as promised, God's eternal and unconditional love for His people remained constant, and His presence never left them. Forty-two generations after Abraham was called out from Ur of the Chaldeans came Messiah Yeshua—that Unique Individual; the Ancient of Days who existed from the beginning; the One who was divine yet went through the human birthing process and was born to Joseph and Miriam, a son and daughter from the line of Judah.

HUMILITY AS A BRIDGE

Rabbi Shaul (Paul) speaks of humbling ourselves to the point of sacrificial love. He uses the example of the Teacher coming down to us as God and man simultaneously. In order to have a "ministry of reconciliation," our priority must be to honor others above ourselves. How else can we be a strong chain of brothers and sisters joined together under the tallit of Hashem as an echad? Yeshua is the bridge who links us mutually.

For all my thirty years in ministry, I have been labeled as a "peacemaker" and have led numerous mediations between leaders, congregants, and couples who needed counseling. I consider this opportunity a wonderful gift from Adonai. He is the One who has put a passion for reconciliation in my heart. I make an effort to humble myself in all situations for the sake of peace. Remember, as discussed previously, humility is not weakness; it shows great strength to surrender your will to Yeshua. Nevertheless, sometimes a situation is so grueling that, no matter how relentlessly you strive, the other person's behavior is so egregious that the motive of the individual's heart must be amiss.

Only Hashem can change someone's prideful and mendacious intentions. In those situations all you can do is shake the dust off your shoes and pray the person gets a touch from Yeshua. Conversely, most of the mediations, though heart-wrenching in the beginning when both parties were not walking with the Teacher, have ended in peace, reconciliation, and love, to the glory of Shaddai!

UNITY IN MARRIAGE

God created the institution of marriage in the Garden of Eden as a union between a man and a woman. When the Pharisees asked the Teacher if it is permitted for a man to divorce his wife for any reason, He answered by first reminding them of what was instituted by God in the Gan

Eden. Then He spoke of how a married couple is no longer two but one flesh (basar echad).

Yeshua then said:

> "Therefore what God has joined together, let no man separate." They said to Him, "Why then did Moses command to 'give her a certificate of divorce and put her away'?" *Yeshua* said to them, "Because of your hardness of heart Moses permitted you to divorce your wives, but from the beginning it was not so."
>
> —MATTHEW 19:6–8

This hardness of the heart can be traced back to the Gan Eden when both man and woman disobeyed Hashem and fell into deception. The Teacher shows us that pride must not enter into our marriage. In God's love we must prioritize our spouse above ourselves. That is an act of true humility, which Hashem looks upon with gladness and blesses! Marriage is a three-stranded cord, and that third strand, Yeshua, is the bridge to a unified marriage that should not be easily broken.

We see the importance of marriage as the man and woman stand together under the tallit, used to form a chuppah, with the bridesmaids and the parents of the bride on one side and the groomsmen and the parents of the groom on the other side, with both groups standing outside the tallit. As the tzitzit hang down, the two sides are bridged together as one *mishpocha*, one family. Marriage represents the completion of the image of God. It represents the yachad, or the unity or the oneness that Hashem has brought together—the basar echad, the one flesh, the unique composite that results from the coming together of man and woman.

Marriage is a reflection of the echad of the Father; Yeshua, who is Ben Elohim, the Son of God; and the Ruach HaKodesh, all One as we say repeatedly, "ADONAI Eloheinu, ADONAI Echad" (the LORD is our God, the LORD is One). Consequently, our marriage represents our walk with our Teacher. Under the tallit we are bridged together with our spouse. It is no longer about "me"; it is about "us." Selfishness is no longer a valid option. We are called to love our spouse as Yeshua loves us. Yeshua tells us "to do nothing out of selfishness or conceit, but with humility consider others as more important than yourselves" (Phil. 2:3).

The other night I officiated a private wedding. The ceremony was beautiful. The bride and groom stood under the tallit, which represented the covering and presence of God. The Ruach Elohim moved so mightily that after the ceremony all the married couples, Jew and Gentile, black, white, and Hispanic—"one new man" in Messiah— requested that I pray for their marriages. So we all assembled under the tallit, grabbing the "hem of the garment," the tzitzit, as we prayed for strength and healing for all their marriages. The tallit was held high on top of our heads as we experienced His Spirit powerfully. And later on we heard testimonies that healings of marriages took place. The tallit, as the covering of Yeshua, is truly a garment of love!

THE SHABBAT AS A BRIDGE

> So the heavens and the earth were completed along with their entire array. God completed—on the seventh day—His work that He made, and He ceased—on the seventh day—from all His work that He made. Then God blessed the seventh day and sanctified it.
>
> —Genesis 2:1–3

> Though a promise of entering His rest is left open, some of [us] would seem to have fallen short...For we who have trusted are entering into that rest.
>
> —Hebrews 4:1, 3

El Elyon (God Most High) has ordained and sanctified one day every week for us to enter into the tallit of His rest. This does not mean that we cannot rest in Yeshua's presence at any time of any day. We can and should enter that secret place under His tallit every day! Yet according to His Scriptures, He has set a special time for us to come together to rest in His presence as we praise and worship Him.

This is a time when He invites all who are weary and burdened, and promises us rest. He invites us to take His yoke upon us and learn from Him, for He is gentle and humble in heart, and we will find rest for our souls. For His yoke is easy and His burden is light (Matt. 11:28–30). When observed the way it should be, the Shabbat (Sabbath) brings people from all backgrounds, colors, and educational and spiritual strengths into Hashem's presence for us to rest, fellowship, and worship Yeshua together. This fellowship and corporate worship brings unity, which gives us tremendous strength.

THE UNITY OF THE BODY OF MESSIAH

I have often wondered how any individuals or denominations that profess to worship the Jewish Teacher boycott, divest, and put sanctions on anything that has to do with Hashem's children. How can these people and denominations believe that Hashem could ever permanently reject His people and replace them with others? Haven't any of these people read the writings of Rabbi Shaul to the Roman people? "Do not be arrogant, but fear. For if God did not spare the natural branches, neither will He spare you" (Rom. 11:20–21, MEV).

Hashem has made His commands clear. Each of us has to choose whether to accept the truth or reject it. He shows us the way to walk in our everyday life. He tells us to be humble; gentle; patient; and filled with grace, mercy, lovingkindness, forgiveness, truth, godly character, and integrity; and to walk in faith, hope, and His unconditional love. Let us fulfill Yeshua's desire that as a mishpocha (family) we would all be one with Him, the Ruach, and the Father.

CHAPTER 8

PREPARING FOR THE LAST DAYS

THE TALLIT IS a bridge between the ancient past and the prophetic future as we begin to understand Israel's role in God's end-times plan. The world is changing at a faster pace today than at any other time in history. As we study what God's Word has to say about the last days, it seems as though the Scriptures are becoming current headlines. The Bible tells us that in the last days the nations will turn against Israel and it will essentially have to stand on its own (Zech. 14:1–21). In recent years we have seen the United Nations reject Israel,[1] and more and more Christian denominations support the movement to boycott, divest from, and put sanctions on Israel.[2]

Scripture also tells us that in the last days Israel will be attacked from the north (Dan. 11:39–40). That hasn't happened, fortunately, but the United States has given Iran $150 billion despite the fact that its former president threatened to wipe Israel off the map and Iran is known to have nuclear ambitions.[3] The Muslim terrorist group ISIS is recruiting soldiers from around the globe to wage jihad against so-called infidels.[4] And many in America are being called bigots for supporting the biblical institution of marriage.[5]

We have been in the last days since Yeshua said, "I am coming soon" (Rev. 22:7, 20), but current events are causing many people to wonder if Messiah's return is now imminent. What is God telling us about the last days? What will Israel experience? What is in store for the body of Messiah? Where do we even begin to answer these questions? *Kadima!*

The Hebrew word *kadima* (קדימה) means "forward." We must move forward. But in order to know how to move forward in the chaotic days ahead, we must be prepared for what lies before us. These are exciting days for those who are intimate with Hashem because we are marching forward to victory! As Moses and Miriam led the Israelites in the song of victory after crossing the Sea of Reeds and being forever freed from Pharaoh and his chariots, we can sing the song of victory in these days also because we have read the end of the Book and we know that our God reigns!

In the final battle of this age, we read that Yeshua is "clothed in a robe dipped in blood, and the name by which He is called is 'the Word of God'...On His robe and on His thigh He has a name written, 'King of kings, and Lord of lords'" (Rev. 19:13, 16). It would make sense that the robe dipped in blood would be His tallit and the tzitzit. The windings of ten, five, six, five, as discussed in chapter 1, would spell out yod, hey, vav, hey, as we read it from right to left in Hebrew (יהוה). This means "Adonai" or "Lord." The tallit of Messiah will be worn in the final battle, and the Messiah will emerge victorious!

In the Messiah there is victory—not just in the last days, but even now! Shaddai desires for us to trust Him so completely that we are able to sing the song of victory in our daily lives, as Moses and Miriam did, even before we know the outcome of the circumstances we face. We must take on a mind-set of victory, knowing that we are more than conquerors through Him who loved us (Rom. 8:37). Yeshua has won the victory over sin, death, and all the power of the enemy (2 Cor. 2:15). This is the incredible God we serve!

Revelation 19:13 tells us that the One whose robe is

dipped in blood is called the Word of God. When we come under the tallit of Yeshua by choosing to follow Him and obey His Word, we can have confidence that in the end He will cause us to overcome. Often those who trust in Hashem will enter our synagogue burdened with emotional and physical illness, financial and job-related problems, business issues, and so on. But after they enter under the tallit for prayer, they leave excited and encouraged because they know that through Yeshua there is victory over the obstacles they face. When we enter under the tallit in prayer, things may not turn out the way we hoped, but God's power is not limited, and we can trust that "all things work together for good for those who love God, who are called according to His purpose" (Rom. 8:28). Absolutely nothing can separate us from the love of God (Rom. 8:35–39)!

Although the last days will be fraught with wars and tribulation, we can rejoice because they ultimately lead to victory through the Messiah. In the days leading up to Yeshua's return, we must follow His mitzvot (commandments), study His Word, pray, and spread the truth—His message—to as many as we can. Those who have a tallit can wrap themselves in it and listen more carefully to Hashem as they go deeper and deeper into His presence. We are entering times that will bring about the greatest revival in history, one that will cause God's people to return to Him through Yeshua and follow His way, not the way of the world or our own thoughts and imaginations. We do not know the day or the hour God will bring this outpouring. But we know that everything Hashem has prepared before the foundation of the world will be released in its perfect time and season. Hashem is the God of order and perfection.

Many say we are entering the days of Elijah, and that is true, but we must remember that those were days of rebellion, wickedness, idol worship, and defiance of the Word of God. We must be prepared for an increase in physical and spiritual warfare. For Shaddai to raise up an army of formidable and effective soldiers, we must be disciplined, filled with the dunamis (dynamite-like) power of His Spirit, and steadfast in our trust in Hashem and His Word. In order to prepare for the days and be victorious in fulfilling the plans Hashem has for the body of believers in Yeshua, we must alter the way we think.

IT'S TIME FOR NEW JEANS

Did you ever have a pair of pants or a shirt that you had worn for years, and even though it was old and worn, it was so comfortable that you just wore it anyway? I just had to get rid of a pair of jeans like that. They started ripping by my right knee because the material was completely worn out. Initially, at the suggestion of our tailor, I had a patch put on because I was told that is the style today. It looked great! Then, however, the material started to pull away from the patch, and the jeans ripped again. So I tried a second patch. That worked for a while, but then the material pulled away from the second patch.

Consequently, I finally had to do away with the jeans. This reminded me of one of Yeshua's instructions: "No one sews a patch of unshrunk cloth on an old garment. Otherwise the patch pulls away from the old, and a worse tear happens. And no one puts new wine into old wineskins. Otherwise, the wine will burst the skins; and the wine is lost, also the skins. But one puts new wine into fresh wineskins" (Mark 2:21–22).

In order for us to move forward in these coming times of much testing, trials, and tribulations, we must embrace new ways of thinking. We need to renew our minds. The old strategies and methodology won't work. We are in a new era of life in America and the world. Good has become evil, and evil has become good. For those committing acts of terrorism or mass shootings, it is a victory to die while perpetrating such atrocities. This kind of wickedness will only get worse.

As new creations in Messiah, the old wineskins, the old jeans, must go, and we need to get new jeans. We have to fill ourselves with the "new wine" of the Spirit of God. We must be resolute and steadfast in our faith, and we must bring "every thought captive to the obedience of Messiah" (2 Cor. 10:5).

That means we must submit our thoughts and emotions to Yeshua so the adversary doesn't get a chance to deceive us into straying from the Teacher. We must believe God's Word, focus on Him, and make Him the center point of our daily thoughts. We must know the Word of God well enough to be able to compare what is in our minds with what is in the mind of God.

In the days ahead, we will need, as author Francis Frangipane wrote, to "look the impossible straight in the eye and believe God" to demonstrate His power.[6] A friend of mine told my wife and me a story recently about a person who sat next to her on a train. My friend just knew in her spirit that the man was planning some type of evil. With a boldness that could have only come from the Ruach HaKodesh, she looked the man straight in his eyes and shook her head no! She said nothing, but he stood up nervously, got off the train, and ran away.

This woman was wearing her new "jeans" or "wineskins" and was filled with dunamis power from the Spirit, giving her holy boldness and powerful faith. This is what we need as the last days near. In these times we must walk in truth, humility, and the love of Yeshua, yet be bold and willing to operate in the spiritual authority He has given us. We need to be so filled up with His Word and His Spirit that fear and doubt have no other recourse but to flee! We must be like Daniel and trust in Hashem even as we are thrown in the lion's den. This is how we will see victory.

Our trust in Hashem must be more than head knowledge; as Frangipane wrote, we must have our eyes fixed "upon the goodness and power of God so that, no matter what we face outwardly or inwardly, we stand secure."[7]

We are in a war. Our enemy is the adversary of our souls. The mind is a battleground. The devil works to set up strongholds in our minds (of fear, hopelessness, anger, despair, and the like) through his mendacities and deceptions. We must resist him by releasing negative attitudes and self-defeating behaviors and thoughts. We have a choice to make: to pursue victory by receiving God's truth in our hearts and renewing our minds, or to receive defeat by continually executing matters the world's way.

"For though we walk in the flesh, we do not wage war according to the flesh. For the weapons of our warfare are not fleshly but powerful through God for the tearing down of strongholds. We are tearing down false arguments and every high-minded thing that exalts itself against the knowledge of God. We are taking every thought captive to the obedience of Messiah" (2 Cor. 10:3–5). Meditating on the words of Yeshua, the One who is above, and always being thankful to Him are powerful weapons of warfare to renew our minds and build our trust in Him as we choose to pursue victory!

COMMUNING WITH YESHUA

This is why we must come under the tallit and spend time in God's presence. The only way we will be able to forge ahead in the end days and accomplish the work He has for His people to do is to remain in constant fellowship with Yeshua. Under the tallit, as we commune with Him, He pours out His eternal love for us. As problems arise each day, He reminds us that we are His cherished treasure and that He is always with us.

As we pursue this kind of intimacy with Hashem, we must again go back to the garden to understand the roots of this kind of communion. When we read of how Yeshua wants us to be in perfect fellowship with Him, we understand that this fellowship with Him comes from the symbolic drinking of His blood and eating of His body. When we drink of the cup and eat the matzo or unleavened bread of Communion, we acknowledge our faith in Yeshua's atoning sacrifice on the tree (cross). Because we have put our trust in Him, we are permitted to enter the Gan Eden and eat from the Etz Chayim (Tree of

Life)—Yeshua—which enables us to have not only eternal life but also intimate fellowship with Hashem.

Among Jewish followers of Yeshua, this meal of fellowship is repeated every year at the Pesach (Passover) seder, when we remember how God delivered His people from *Mitzrayim* (Egypt). When we drink the third cup of wine in the seder, the cup of Messianic redemption, those who believe in the Teacher are identifying with His blood atonement and are praying for His soon return, and those who are not believers are praying for Mashiach to come. When we partake of the revealed *afikomen* (the unleavened matzo that was hidden and now found), those who believe in Yeshua are identifying with His body that was sacrificed for us and can respond with, "*Dayenu!*" (It is sufficient!). The freedom that we now have as a result of eating from the Tree of Life (Yeshua the Messiah) enables us to enter the paradise of eternal life.

When we come under the tallit as believers in Yeshua, we experience His rest, peace, and stillness. And our ears are more open to hear what His Spirit is saying.

As new creations in Messiah we are delivered from physical and spiritual bondage and allowed to enter the spiritual paradise, where He has given us dominion and authority in Him over all the negative and seducing spirits of deception, lies, anger, bitterness, unforgiveness, and fear. He has given us the *amein* ("so be it," a phrase often said at the end of Jewish prayers), the end, and made us into a new beginning, a *baruch atah* ("blessed are you," a phrase often said at the beginning of Jewish prayers). We are no longer barred by the spiritual flaming swords and can enter into *Kodesh HaKodashim* (the Holy of Holies).

It is in the Kodesh HaKodashim, as we experience the mystery of the prayer shawl, that we meditate upon His Word and worship Him. It is in this time of intimate communion that He gives us words of knowledge and prophecy, and gives us our "marching orders" for each day. The Kodesh HaKodashim is the place where we develop our intimacy with Yeshua. And it is in this place that He empowers us with spiritual gifts that enable us to forge ahead to complete the work He has called us to accomplish.

GOD IS DOING
A NEW THING

Hashem said, "Here I am, doing a new thing; now it is springing up—do you not know about it? I will surely make a way in the desert, rivers in the wasteland" (Isa. 43:19). One new thing we will see is Hashem bringing us together in small groups for discipleship, teaching, prayer, the "breaking of bread," and fellowship, much like it was in the Book of Acts.

The Book of Acts in the B'rit Chadashah speaks about the Ruach HaKodesh empowering the talmidim (disciples) of Yeshua and the thousands of Jewish believers at the Shavuot in Jerusalem. They were all waiting in one accord for His promise after Yeshua ascended to the Father. Rabbi Shaul, thousands and thousands of Jewish believers, and eventually those of other nations who came to believe in the Jewish Messiah desired the fullness of Yeshua's promise, the immersion in the Ruach HaKodesh.

In the end days we are going to experience the supernatural with miracles, signs, and wonders, just as they did in Acts—and all who put their trust in Him will see even greater signs, as Yeshua promised. A message of repentance will be boldly preached before powerful leaders, governments, and worldwide institutions and organizations. Multitudes will hear the call and respond with repentance and confession. Masses will be healed! The name of Yeshua will be proclaimed worldwide. Mysteries of ages past will be unlocked. The body of Messiah will stand with Israel and the Jewish people. In Acts we see a tremendous and unbelievable transformation from fear and doubt to the fullness of power and fire of God's Spirit flowing out to His shlichim (apostles) so they could spread the good news of Yeshua to the world! We will see the same again soon.

THE SPIRIT OF AMALEK

In the troubled and chaotic times that await us, there will be great happenings, multitudes of blessings, times of peace and prosperity, and a powerful exercising of the gifts of the Ruach. But there also will be dismal failures, poverty, an increase in strange and threatening weather patterns, increased terrorism, and wars and rumors of war. When Israel was in the wilderness, they were always quarreling against Moses for bringing them out of Egypt. They followed Moses, but their faith in Hashem was vacillating, even after all the miraculous victories they had witnessed. Their response to the meeting of their needs was to question whether God was with them. Their trust in Him was almost nonexistent.

Most of the nations were fearful of the God of Israel,

but the Amalekites were not. Consequently, they attacked Israel at Rephidim. They began their attack in the rear against the elderly and feeble. Joshua led the battle as Moses stood on top of the hill.

When Moses's hands were lifted up high as in praise to God, there was victory. But when he got tired and lowered them, the people of Israel began losing the battle. Seeing this pattern, Aaron and Hur went up the hill and put down a stone for Moses to sit on, and they held up his hands, one on each side. As long as Moses's hands were lifted up, there was victory! Then Adonai told Moses, "'Write this for a memorial in the book, and rehearse it in the hearing of Joshua, for I will utterly blot out the memory of the Amalekites from under heaven.' Then Moses built an altar, and called the name of it *ADONAI-Nissi* [God is my banner]'" (Exod. 17:14–15).

Adonai then declared that He would have war with Amalek from generation to generation. In the last days the spirit of Amalek will continue to rear its ugly head with a renewed rise of anti-Semitism. This anti-Messiah spirit will again attempt to destroy the Jewish people. Unfortunately, this has already begun, even in the body of Messiah, as some denominations refuse to stand with the nation of Israel.

In the last days there will be vicious attacks worldwide against the Jewish people and Jewish communities everywhere. Israel will be attacked by its enemies and will suffer some death and destruction, but the people of Israel will call out to Adonai, and He will have compassion on them, and Israel will be victoriously vindicated as Adonai Elohim is glorified! As the prophet Zechariah declared, when the nations gather against Jerusalem to wage war, "ADONAI will go forth and fight against those nations as He fights in a day of battle" (Zech. 14:2–3).

Years ago there were signs in Israel declaring, "First they will come for the Saturday people (the Jewish people) and then they will come for the Sunday people (Christians)." There are already attacks against Israel, but we are also seeing a spiritual war between the God of Israel and the god of secularism (the deification of man). That is the force behind efforts to remove the Ten Commandments from government buildings and to prohibit prayer in public schools. People want to rely solely on man's strength and wisdom, and they are aggressively resisting divine authority. The good news is that the God of Abraham, Isaac, and Jacob will reign supreme. There will again be, as in the Hanukkah battle over three thousand years ago, victory for the "sons of Zion" (those who worship the God of Abraham, Isaac, and Jacob) over the "sons of Greece" (those who worship the god of self), and hearts will be turned toward Yeshua.

In the Tanakh Hashem promises that He will fill us up so that we can experience His awesome, miracle-working power in the end days: "So it will be afterward, I will pour out My *Ruach* on all flesh: your sons and daughters will prophesy, your old men will dream dreams, your young men will see visions. Also on the male and the female servants will I pour out My spirit in those days. I will show wonders in the heavens and on the earth...Then all who call on ADONAI's Name will escape [be delivered or saved]" (Joel 3:1–3, 5).

This prophecy from *Yoel haNavi*, Joel the prophet, was

delivered sometime between 500 and 800 BC and spoke of what was to take place in the last days of civilization as we know it today. This prophecy was also spoken in the Book of Acts at that Shavuot when the Ruach was given. The key to their receiving the outpouring given then and 1,500 years previously at Mount Sinai was that they were all in one accord. When the body of Messiah is together in one accord, we will receive the amazing favor of God, as was experienced at Sinai and among the believers at the beginning of Acts.

When we are in unity and can humble ourselves before one another by not focusing on the blemishes and imperfections of our neighbors but on their good and positive attributes, then we are following Yeshua's commandment to love God with all our heart, soul, and strength, and to love our neighbors as ourselves. This unity pleases Yeshua and moves His heart to give us prophetic revelation. And it allows Him to open our eyes to the supernatural kingdom of the Most High (El Elyon).

Hashem created us so that we may praise, worship, and fellowship with Him for all eternity. He has created a people for Himself, but all things that are created have a beginning and an end. Our time on earth is limited, but the spirit He gives us when we are conceived will live for eternity with or without Him. He gives us the time we are on earth to decide which it will be.

Choosing Yeshua means making intimate fellowship with Him a priority. It means spending quiet time in His presence. Enter under the tallit and be empowered with spiritual gifts from Yeshua. There is so much work to be done that we need to get stronger and stronger in Him.

He commissioned Israel to be a kingdom of priests and a holy nation through the Teacher. If you are a follower of Yeshua, He has commissioned you to take His message of salvation, deliverance, healing, and the resultant joy to the Jewish people and to the nations. In order to fulfill this commission, we will speak the message of Yeshua "not with persuasive words of wisdom, but in demonstration of the Spirit and of power—so that [their] faith would not be in the wisdom of men but in the power of God" (1 Cor. 2:4–5).

A RADICAL REVIVAL

As Yeshua spreads out His tallit upon all who believe in Him, there will be a crossing over of cultures, languages, and traditions. Under His tallit we will come together as one. Adonai had to separate humankind in ancient Babylon when they attempted to build a tower to heaven, but in the last days He will bring us together in one accord as the god of secularism is defeated. Fear, pride, and passivity are enemies of growth; in the last days there will be a forward movement, kadima, and breakthrough. This is because, as we come together under Yeshua's tallit, He will look with favor upon us and transform us into dynamos of spiritual impact. Together we will become the "one new man" prophesied by Rabbi Shaul (Eph. 2:15).

As I place myself under the tallit of Mashiach, I think of the most radical act I ever committed in my life, which was to allow Yeshua, the Teacher and Messiah, to enter my heart. In time I have come to know many people who were born Jewish and embraced Yeshua as Messiah. But as we near the last days, the number of Jewish believers in Yeshua will grow exponentially.

The greatest revival in history will take place among the Jewish people, and Hashem will use the Messianic Jewish people as His vessels:

> Thus says ADONAI-Tzva'ot, "In those days it will come to pass that ten men from every language of the nations will grasp the corner of the garment [tallit] of a Jew saying, 'Let us go with you, for we have heard that God is with you.'"
> —ZECHARIAH 8:23

The Jewish people have a prophetic call to be radical, as I was when I embraced Yeshua as Messiah. Just as it was two thousand years ago when the first Messianic rabbis transformed the whole world, so will it be in the end days. Whole cities are named after the early Messianic Jewish rabbis because of the profound impact they made. It is as Hashem said through the prophet Zechariah: "Then I will pour out on the house of David and the inhabitants of Jerusalem a spirit of grace and supplication, when they will look toward Me whom they pierced. They will mourn for him as one mourns for an only son and grieve bitterly for him, as one grieves for a firstborn" (Zech. 12:10).

The prophet Isaiah also declared, "It will come to pass in the last days that the mountain of ADONAI's House will stand firm as head of the mountains and will be exalted above the hills. So all nations will flow to it. Then many peoples will go and say: 'Come, let us go up to the mountain of ADONAI, to the House of the God of Jacob! Then

He will teach us His ways, and we will walk in His paths.'
For *Torah* will go forth from Zion and the word of ADONAI
from Jerusalem" (Isa. 2:2–3).

Let us also not forget that 12,000 from every tribe
except the tribe of Dan—or 144,000—will have the seal of
God marked on their foreheads as servants of El Elyon,
the Most High God! As the body of Messiah sees millions
of the Jewish people receive their Messiah, the nations
will be provoked to jealousy, and we will see the greatest
revival to ever take place.

> Then all the survivors from all the nations that
> attacked Jerusalem will go up from year to year
> to worship the King, ADONAI-*Tzva'ot*, and to cele-
> brate *Sukkot*. Furthermore, if any of the nations on
> earth do not go up to Jerusalem to worship the King,
> ADONAI-*Tzva'ot*, they will have no rain.
>
> —ZECHARIAH 14:16–17

The intentions of our hearts as Jewish people will be
restored to true worship of Adonai, and we will be vessels
of glory to the nations. As the Teacher has taught us, we
will all declare, "*Shema Yisrael ADONAI Eloheinu ADONAI
Echad, ADONAI Hu HaElohim. Yeshua et ADONAI!*" (Hear
O Israel, the LORD is our God, the LORD is One. The LORD,
He is God. Yeshua is the LORD!)

THE SPIRIT OF PROPHECY

As this era begins to close, Hashem's eternal love and desire
that none should perish shall result in an unleashing of

His spiritual gifts of authority, boldness, favor, and preternatural vision that no eye has seen, no ear has heard, and no heart can ever comprehend the awesomeness of His majestic, eternal divinity.

"The testimony of *Yeshua* is the Spirit of Prophecy" (Rev. 19:10). And the tallit of Yeshua symbolizes the Spirit of prophecy. As we enter under Yeshua's tallit, we bridge the past to the future as we understand Israel's prophetic role in God's plan in the last days. Under the tallit things begin to make sense. Hashem opens up to us fresh revelations of His Word. It is a time of supernatural and always-expanding learning and intimacy with the promised Messiah.

Hashem has an eternal love for you. And if you open your heart to the supernatural; to signs, wonders, and miracles; to the impossible as opposed to your intellectual reasoning; then you will find the possible in that which transcends all time, light, energy, dimension, and space.

CONCLUSION

O N THAT BEAUTIFUL summer day in August of 1963, a few weeks before my fourteenth birthday, I had no idea that a conversation with two friends would lead me on a spiritual search for truth. That journey ultimately led me to the Teacher, Yeshua HaMashiach, and unearthed other treasures that help us answer the mystifying questions about the reason for our existence. The tallit, a foremost treasure, symbolically speaks of the calling of God; humility; the covering of God; God's presence, power, and protection; healing; forgiveness; faith; prayer and meditation; loving-kindness and generosity; integrity and good character; and unity—the spiritual tools needed in the coming days.

I have written about the significance of the tallit in the life cycle of events, and the meanings, myths, and mysteries surrounding the prayer shawl. I have written about the tallit as a picture of Israel and Yeshua, and how it points to the true God of all creation. Nevertheless, the greatest mystery of the prayer shawl is how it brings us into intimate fellowship with the Master of all creation, the One who is our *Yedid Nefesh*, the lover of our souls; the One who was, who is, and who is to come.

I challenge you to enter the secret place under the tallit. Allow it to remind you of His presence and His Word and the price Yeshua paid so you could commune with Him. Be still and know that He is God. Experience the healing in His wings. Ask Him to fill you with His Ruach HaKodesh so you can walk in holy boldness and dunamis power. Ask Him to empower you with His spiritual gifts so you can accomplish all that He created you to do. And ask Him to show you the mystery of the prayer shawl and to open your eyes to His many spiritual treasures.

Hashem has an eternal, matchless love for you. His banner—His tallit—over you is love (Song of Sol. 2:4). Get to know Him intimately under the tallit. Dwell in the shelter of the Most High; "under His wings [His tallit] you will find refuge" (Ps. 91:4).

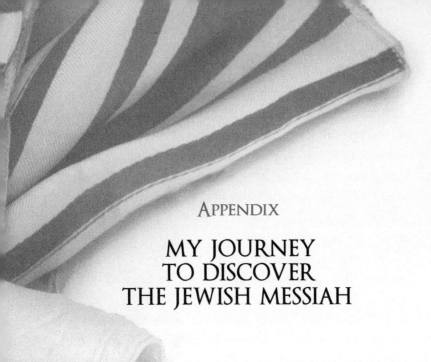

APPENDIX

MY JOURNEY TO DISCOVER THE JEWISH MESSIAH

F ROM THE MOMENT we are born, each one of us travels on a different path. Each one of us makes a choice at some time in life, whether knowingly or unknowingly, as to which road we shall follow. As we walk down the path we have chosen, God drops love notes to us. When our spiritual eyes are opened, we understand His love notes and we choose to follow the course He has chosen for our lives.

That is what happened to me. I was raised to respect Hashem, but "Jesus" was not a name we uttered in my home. My father knew God and loved God. He grew up as a "conservadox" Jew, practicing something between Conservative and Orthodox Judaism. He graduated with a degree in pharmacy from Columbia University in 1933 and owned several pharmacies in stores throughout New York City. As a professional man he was a person of integrity, and he served in and led many professional, community, and religious organizations. Like his parents and his two sisters, my father loved God and loved the Jewish people, religion, customs, and traditions.

My parents married in 1940. My mother came from a secular Jewish family. When my sister and I came along, my father made sure the Jewish religion, customs, and culture were a major part of our family life. Wanting to ensure that I would love God and God's people, my father taught me at the age of five to pray the Shema (which begins, "Hear, O Israel, the LORD is our God, the LORD is One") every night before I went to sleep and then to pray for my family and talk to God.

At five years old, without a clue as to what I was doing, I innocently and willingly began the spiritual journey that

I truly believe had been planned by Hashem. Every night I would go to sleep praying the Shema and communicating with the Creator of all there is. When I was upset with someone in my family, I would omit their names that night from prayer. That was my way of communicating my feelings with my Abba (Daddy) in heaven.

Like other Jewish boys, when I was thirteen I had my bar mitzvah, where I received a new tallit. For many people, their religious studies and commitments end when they finish celebrating after their bar/bat mitzvah. But that was not the way with me. I decided to study Jewish history and observances for another two years. During that time I even led the liturgy with my rabbi at a special Shabbat service. Of course, as is customary, I did all of these while wearing a tallit.

Then one day in 1964, a friend I'll call Bobby and I went to the New York World's Fair. We both had been there multiple times before, but this time there was something new that absolutely intrigued me. I loved all of the pavilions, especially those that showed some of the new devices and machines that were being proposed for the future. But there was one pavilion that seemed to have the longest line. It was the Billy Graham pavilion. I wondered who Billy Graham was and why so many people were waiting for hours to get into his pavilion. So I said to my friend, "Let's try to get in and find out what it's all about."

We did not want to wait in line, so we found a fence, jumped over it, and snuck in! We had no idea what they were speaking about, but there was some prayer they told us we could pray aloud with them if we wanted to do so. I prayed out loud what they spoke, and then as part of the prayer I said the words "Jesus Christ."

That night when I prayed the Shema, I asked God to forgive me for saying the worst words that could ever be mentioned. I didn't really know what I had done, but I felt that it was the worst thing possible. So I begged God for forgiveness, though I didn't know why.

That experience was still at the back of my mind three years later when I experienced severe physical and emotional trauma. In July 1967 I was in a terrible car accident. I was in the hospital for about ten days and then spent a little more than a month recuperating. Then four months later, my father passed away. (I discovered many years later that he had come to believe in Yeshua the Messiah before he died.) I decided to honor his memory by attending a synagogue service every Shabbat for most of the year. In hindsight I can see that God was working all these things together for my good, as Romans 8:28 says, because those experiences caused me to think even more about the God of Israel.

The following year I transferred to the University of Buffalo, where my spiritual journey intensified. I wanted to try anything that I thought would enable me to experience deeper introspection and eventually lead me to God. There was an evangelist (at that time I had no clue what that word even meant) who regularly came into my girlfriend's dorm. He was so happy and filled with peace. He spoke to us about God and Yeshua, and was always asking people if they knew where they would go when they died. We mocked him and said things like, "We don't want to go anywhere but to never-never land, so we don't get old and die." But his question did make me think.

I decided to visit various spiritual groups where I could meditate, smell incense, and seek God. One time, I remember going to a Hare Krishna meeting and thinking the group was named after Harry Krischner, a successful Jewish businessman. I thought the meeting might be good since Harry Krischner was successful and loads of Jewish students attended. Well, I found neither God there nor the successful Jewish businessman.

AN ENCOUNTER
WITH THE MESSIAH

In 1972, when I was traveling cross-country from New York to California and then back to New York, I made a stop at the Mormon Tabernacle and saw a film on Joseph Smith. I didn't believe he was the Messiah, but I told the person I was with, "Every religion has its Messiah-type person. For the Christians, it is Jesus. So maybe Yeshua is *a* Messiah, *a* Lamb of God."

The Torah says in the Book of Exodus, "Tell all the congregation of Israel that on the tenth day of this month, each man is to take a lamb for his family one lamb for the household" (Exod. 12:3). At that point the Teacher became to me a messiah, a lamb of God.

From 1974 to 1993, I was mostly in practice as an optometrist, specializing in children's and sports vision. In 1976, I opened a private practice in Pembroke Pines, Florida. I had a friend I'll call Jim who was in a related profession. We would often refer patients to each other.

When I met Jim and his wife, Diane, I found them to be very unique. Their lives were all about Yeshua. They acknowledged Him in everything they did. There was something different about them, and I wanted to know what it was. They told me about how they grew up Catholic but later came to really know the Messiah. Nothing they said made sense to me, but they made me want to continue my search for God.

After we'd had a business relationship for a while, Jim and Diane introduced me to another couple who became wonderful friends. He was born Jewish and she was not, but their whole lives were all about Yeshua. They communicated with Yeshua every day of their lives in prayer, and I learned years later that they prayed for a list of Jewish friends who needed to meet their Messiah. My name was on that list, and they prayed for me daily for years.

One night in 1978, Jim and Diane invited me to their house for dinner. We had great conversations and a great dinner. We spoke a little bit about business, but most of our discussions centered on Yeshua the Teacher. After dinner I was sitting on a couch in their living room while they cleaned up in the kitchen. As we were talking, something supernatural occurred. All of a sudden, a strong, warm feeling of love, peace, and extreme comfort and security fell upon me. I had never felt this way before. It was such a unique experience that I stood up from where I was sitting on their couch and said, "You're right! Yeshua is the Messiah!"

Jim and Diane looked quizzically at me because they hadn't seen or felt what I had experienced. Why was I saying Yeshua was the Messiah?

At that time another scripture from the Torah became a reality to me: "But if the household is too small for a lamb, then he and his nearest neighbor are to take one according to the number of the people. According to each person eating, you are to make your count for the lamb" (Exod. 12:4). Yeshua became the Passover Lamb to me—the Messiah. However, this was just coming from my intellect, not my spirit.

My new friendships reinspired me to continue my search for God. I wanted to know Him. I believed Yeshua was the Messiah, but I didn't know what difference that was supposed to make. I started reading books about aliens (Robert Heinlein's *Stranger in a Strange Land*); people who had supposedly died and then returned; and the mysteries of life such as the Bermuda Triangle, Area 51, Stonehenge, the Egyptian pyramids, the Moai of Easter Island, the Nazca Lines of Peru, and Atlantis and other mysterious civilizations. One of my favorite books was *Chariots of the Gods? Unsolved Mysteries of the Past* by Erich von Däniken.

I even tried Eastern chanting because I was told it would draw you closer to God and bring blessings in your life. I was on a B'nai B'rith bowling team and meditated on certain words each time I got up to bowl. It didn't work! I was also on a B'nai B'rith softball team. I didn't chant before or during the games, and I played better than I bowled!

Over the next few years as I continued my search for God, I told people that I believed Yeshua was the Messiah, but I did not think of Him as my Messiah. I was the president of my local B'nai B'rith and president-elect of my local optometric association. I was also politically involved in Broward County, so I had a busy life. Then in December 1981, a beautiful young Jewish redhead brought her twelve-year-old child into my office for a developmental vision exam. Immediately we each knew we had found the love of our lives. On our very first date, I told this wonderful woman that I believed Yeshua was the Messiah. But we were in love, so it didn't matter to her what I said!

We got married seven months later on July 10, 1982. We had about one hundred people in our condo in Plantation, Florida. It was a beautiful time of fellowship with delicious food, and it was written about in our local newspaper. However, during the ceremony, a supernatural event took place. The rabbi was leading the ceremony and we were covered in my tallit, as is traditionally done during Jewish weddings. As we were reciting the wedding vows and Hebrew prayers to each other, the sky lit up with lightning and there was a loud crash of thunder. We were in Florida, where rainstorms are fairly common, but the thunder and lightning occurred only at that special time in the ceremony. The skies were clear, and the weather was otherwise beautiful. We believed God was blessing our marriage, and then we witnessed a true personal supernatural miracle later that night that probably became the cornerstone of our spiritual journey and the sign that Yeshua was indeed with us!

A REVELATION
OF THE LAMB

Happily married, my wife and I just enjoyed being in each other's company. We were both very involved in the community, socially and politically. But none of our activities brought us any closer to finding God.

My wife and I belonged to a temple and enjoyed our participation in the religious community. One day we decided to ask our rabbi how we could know God. He said, "Stick around because I will speak about God once or twice this year in my sermons." That didn't do it for us. So we went from synagogue to synagogue, denomination to denomination, searching for God's Spirit. We loved our Judaism; we loved our Jewish life; we loved celebrating our Jewish traditions and our Jewish people. But we wanted more. We wanted to know God!

Then in 1985, we went to a baby-naming ceremony that was being held in a church. We had been in that church previously, but this time as we entered the sanctuary, the Spirit of God fell upon us in a most magnificent and supernatural way. This happened to both of us at the same moment. For two and a half hours we wept and wept. Both of us heard the voice of God speaking to our spirits, and we heard the exact same words: "I am God. Jesus [the Teacher] is My Son. The Bible is true. Come follow Me." As we both wept, my wife asked, "How am I going to tell my mother?" At that time, another Torah scripture became a reality to me: "Your lamb is to be without blemish, a year old male. You may take it from the sheep or from the

179

goats" (Exod. 12:5). In that moment, Yeshua became *my* Lamb, *my* Messiah!

For years I had been searching for God. I didn't just want to know about Him—I wanted to know Him intimately. I wondered if this were even possible. Could mankind ever know the intimate workings of God? Would He be the best possible Father in all of creation? Would He love me, and was I capable of loving Him?

My father was a wonderful man. He was a great father, husband, friend, employer, and leader. Wherever he went, he was known and loved. But he was only human. The Father of all creation loves us eternally. Even as we sin and need to repent, His love never wavers!

As my wife and I came to know Yeshua and studied God's Word, we received the fullness of His Ruach HaKodesh—His Holy Spirit. We developed intimacy with Him, and our questions began to be answered.

OUR LIVES TURNED UPSIDE DOWN

Having the Messiah in our hearts produced a major change in our lives. My wife began going by her Hebrew name, רחל, spelling it *Racquel*, and has been doing so for the last twenty-five years. We were neither prepared for nor desired a change. Our lives were good. We were in love with each other and had been in a great marriage for over three years. We were both professionals with successful practices; involved professionally, politically, and socially in our community; and wanted that *kesher*—that connection—to the one who has created all that there is.

But all of a sudden our lives were turned upside down. We studied and studied the Word of God. Instead of reading all the books that supposedly explained the unsolved mysteries of life, we decided to read and study the number-one best seller of all time—the Bible—from Genesis (Bereishit) to Revelation! Along with reading the Word, I studied rabbinic and Christian commentaries and delved into many of the Jewish writings of antiquity. It was the Jewish writings that helped solidify my belief in Yeshua the Teacher, because the writings of old made me even more convinced that He was truly the Messiah, the One for whom Israel has been looking.

Our lives were turned upside down because the focus of our lives had changed. We kept reality-checking ourselves so that we knew beyond a shadow of a doubt that we weren't just mesmerized and believing some ridiculous, cultic ideas. We were surrounded by many good friends and professional acquaintances, and fortunately we had a great family. We were admired and well respected. However, we found out quickly that our friends and family would support us in anything we wanted to pursue except one thing. This one thing transformed us from people who were loved and well liked to "lepers." A rabbi with whom I had been friends for years heard about my new faith and decided to write me a letter and tell me that I had been "duped." He told me not to return to temple until I could say I was wrong and apologize.

I was flabbergasted! I thought that if he believed I was doing something so terrible, he would want to counsel me and help me get back on the right path. His was not an offer to restore one who had strayed; it was a total rejection. I knew this was not like the Teacher. Yeshua would lovingly show me where I had gone wrong and keep speaking to me until I either heard His voice or made up my mind to reject His Word. But in my circle of family and friends, no crime or life change would isolate you more than to follow Yeshua. Religious men would "rend their garments" and mourn for their children if they decided to follow the Teacher.

To borrow a line from Bob Dylan, how many roads must we walk down before we will believe? There is only one road that leads to truth. It is the road to knowing the *Adon Olam* (אדון עולם), the eternal Lord, through knowing His Messiah, Yeshua.

Part of the process of having our lives turned upside down was finding a new place to worship. We went to a church for a very short time, but the culture was so very different from the Jewish synagogues we had been attending. We now believed in the Jewish Messiah. Yeshua was a Jew and followed the Torah perfectly. This means that He had to wear a tallit or tallit gadol (large tallit) every day of His life, and we know He did so because He followed every commandment. He was born as a Jew, He lived as a Jew, and He died as a Jew. His mother, Miriam (Mary), gave Him a Jewish name, Yeshua (Jesus), which means "salvation."

At the church, three things happened that made us feel uncomfortable. First, the pastor told us that if we would empty our checkbook and give in faith, we would receive an amazing blessing. I am a businessman and desire a good investment when I see it. If this was what Yeshua was telling me to do, I would believe it. However, this whole idea of believing in Yeshua was so foreign to me that I decided to try it in faith and see what would happen.

Well, it didn't work out quite the way the pastor said it would, but I did get to have a great conversation with the president of my bank, who called to tell me that there wasn't enough money in my account to cover some of the checks I had written. Thank God I was able to run over to the bank so I could pay the difference and not be penalized! The interesting thing is that even though this whole faith concept was so foreign to me, my experience of coming to know Yeshua was so great that I truly believed and was willing to do whatever He said.

The second uncomfortable experience was at a men's fellowship breakfast that I attended after going to the church for a few weeks. I sat at a table and had no problem talking to all the men about my new experience with Yeshua. I compared this new spiritual existence with the movie *Oh, God!*, which stars George Burns and John Denver. As an assistant grocery manager (John Denver) is doing his job, a good-natured old man (George Burns) appears as the almighty God and selects him as his messenger for the modern world. To me, it was a great comparison to what God had done in our lives. However, before I could finish my testimony, some of the men at the table interrupted me and said I should not be going to the movies because it wasn't right according to God's Word. I didn't get a chance to say anything more about what God had done in our lives. Consequently, when I went home I told my wife that I didn't think we should attend the church anymore because the culture was too foreign. She was in total agreement with me.

The third uncomfortable situation was that the men's fellowship breakfast was on a Saturday. It didn't feel right to me to attend a function in a religious institution on a Saturday. I felt that if I were going to attend a religious gathering on a Saturday, I should be in a synagogue. Again, it is not that there is anything wrong with being in a church, but it was foreign to my culture. No one was wearing a tallit, and to make matters worse, I was served ham and eggs. I felt that if I was going to follow Yeshua, then I should follow the Word He wrote. I ended up not eating the breakfast and going home hungry. But I did believe I had done what Yeshua wanted me to do.

COMING HOME

About a month later, in January of 1986, Racquel and I decided to visit Temple Aron HaKodesh (TAK) in Fort Lauderdale. We had felt so out of place in the church we had been attending, but when we walked through the doors of TAK, it was as if the walls grabbed us and the Spirit of God said, "You are home." It was the most magnificent feeling. There were men and women of all ages from the United States, Israel, and many other nations, all singing, dancing, and rejoicing in God through Yeshua. And the men were wearing tallitot, just as the Teacher did!

We were greeted by a Holocaust survivor and her husband, and were welcomed by others with great excitement and rejoicing. They had a rabbi, an assistant rabbi, and a cantor, who all wore tallitot. There was an ark with a Torah inside, and there was an American and an Israeli flag up on the *bimah*, which is a raised platform in a synagogue that contains the ark, the Torah, and the reading table used when chanting or reading portions of the Torah and the Prophets.

I had visited TAK twice, once in 1978 and once in 1980, before I was a believer in Yeshua. This visit to TAK was different. The almighty God, the Teacher, the Ruach HaKodesh (Holy Spirit), all part of the one true God, the Echad (One) in the Shema, came to hug us and welcome us home! Finally things began to feel "right"!

Racquel and I began attending TAK on a regular basis. It was different from non-Messianic Judaism, but it was a wonderful experience. It was there that we learned to worship God, pray for people, and experience the awesome presence of the Most High God.

We realized that we had been performing certain rituals without really understanding what we were doing. This is common in Judaism. You complete the required rituals and then you learn why. For example, I never really knew the meaning of the tallit, but I would wear it because I was supposed to wear it. As a matter of fact, I never could have dreamed of all the spiritual treasures you can receive from it, which I shared in this book. Most of all, I learned that the Messiah of Israel wore the tallit every day, and I came to the realization that everyone who believes in Yeshua and desires to wear a tallit can do so as long as they understand and respect its holiness, whether they were born Jewish or not.

We knew we were supposed to have a *mikveh* (ritual water immersion in Judaism), so we were told to bring a bathing suit and a T-shirt to cover ourselves. Remember, we had come to know the Teacher only three months earlier. As we had been used to, we both wore bikini type bathing suits, and I wore a T-shirt from our honeymoon that said, "I got *lei'd* in Hawaii"! Needless to say, the leaders had a big chuckle from our spiritual and ritual innocence!

The assistant rabbi began to disciple us on a weekly basis. When he asked us what God was asking us to do to serve Him, we gave a list about a page long. He responded by telling us that we must discover His priority for us. Soon, God began to narrow our focus. After studying the Jewish roots of the Teacher relentlessly, within six months I was teaching a weekly study at my house. It turned out to be very successful and drew close to ninety singles. As a result, the rabbis were excited and "raised" (or selected) my wife and me to be the singles leaders of the synagogue.

The "raising up" experience was quite interesting. The rabbis said that I should invite my mother, who was living in the next town, to the synagogue for our Friday night service so she could watch us be "raised up." Racquel and I had no clue as to what that meant, but we knew it was something good.

In the midst of the Erev Shabbat (Sabbath evening) service we were called up to the bimah so the rabbis and elders could "lay hands" on us, meaning they prayed for us and anointed us to lead the singles ministry as Moses and Aaron did to those raised up to be leaders in the Torah. There were beautiful prayers and prophetic "words of knowledge" spoken over us. This was all new to us, but we came to understand that words of knowledge are messages of divine instruction that are received in the spirit realm from God through the Ruach Hakodesh, or Holy

Spirit. When Racquel and I sat down next to my mother she said, "That was very nice. So when are they going to raise you up?" We told her, "We think it just occurred!"

I am fortunate that my mother also came to know Yeshua as her Messiah and spent many years growing in intimacy with Him before she died.

FROM DOCTOR TO RABBI

Before long I noticed that I was spending more and more time studying, teaching, and serving in the temple and less time in my practice. When a door opened, I would tell my patients about the spiritual treasures I was finding in Hashem, but my heart was turning more and more toward ministry. The singles ministry was growing, and Racquel and I were doing lots of counseling and discipleship.

Eventually the rabbi gave me a small office in the temple. Soon it was clear that my heart was no longer in my field of optometry or in my practice. I felt a calling to become a Messianic rabbi. At first I didn't tell anyone, but when I mentioned it to Racquel, she was in total agreement with me. I soon began to work just part time in the medical practice and volunteered more and more in the temple.

That decision took a major toll on our finances because I saw very few patients. A very embarrassing experience occurred during that season. Someone knew I was struggling financially, so he gave my name to a church that gave a turkey and cartons of food to needy families at Thanksgiving. That Thanksgiving, they came to the gate of our condo and asked the guard, who had attended our wedding, for Dr. Kluge. When the doorbell rang, I was blessed but terribly humbled. I thank God for His faithfulness! The food was a welcome blessing.

After a season of heart-wrenching difficulties, God began to bless us. Opportunities opened up, and I was able to see more patients on a part-time basis. The transition from doctor to rabbi taught me how to depend on our God Most High! Not only did He provide for us financially, but He also opened doors for us to minister. He gave us an opportunity to pray with a terminally ill neighbor who had been rejecting prayer because it seemed the individuals who had visited him were only interested in converting him from Judaism. Hashem created a tremendous open door for us to minister to him, and the man received Yeshua into his heart just a few days before he died. He also gave us an opportunity to tell people about the Teacher on our friend's television program, and in time we began to travel to speak at conferences.

By 1989, I had been ordained as a Messianic rabbi. I had been transitioning from a full-time medical practice to full-time volunteer minister for a few years. One day during a weekly staff meeting, we discussed the need for someone to begin a Bible study in the West Palm Beach area. The temple leaders knew God had someone for the job but couldn't discern who that was. After prayer and discussion, we realized the person was me! It was my time to go to the West Palm Beach area and begin a study.

When my wife and I were called forward to be anointed to lead this Bible study by the laying on of hands, the three other rabbis who were praying for us kept making reference to a new congregation. Later, I asked the three other rabbis why they kept mentioning a new congregation when it was just a new study group we were leading. We all agreed that Ruach HaKodesh was speaking through them, and consequently the vision for a new synagogue was conceived! After fourteen months of preparation, in January 1991, we were "sent out" with prayer, fasting, and the blessing of the leaders of TAK to begin a new synagogue.

On February 14, 1991, Melech Israel was born. The name was shortly changed to Melech Yisrael. For the next two years I was in full-time ministry and seeing patients part time in the West Palm Beach and Fort Lauderdale areas. We moved from Boca Raton to Palm Beach Gardens in 1991 and then in 1993, I retired from practice to concentrate on the one thing to which Yeshua was calling me: ministry as a Messianic rabbi.

We are all searching for life's meaning! Deep down, in the inner recesses of our hearts (our *kishkes*), we all desire to know our purpose. This can be revealed only through a spiritual journey. The Shema and the tallit were just the beginning of my understanding my need for Hashem, but the fullness of my relationship with Him came from the Teacher, and I continued to grow in Him as I walked with Him and studied His Word.

As we uncover the other treasures that Hashem lets us find, His purpose for us begins to come to the light. Did I ever imagine that I would, at the age of thirty-six, transition from helping people to see and focus in the natural realm to helping them to see and focus in the spiritual realm? The answer is a resounding, "No!" However, when you seek to know God, you will find Him, and He will make His purpose for your life crystal clear.

Each one of us is searching to discover the hidden treasures of life. We may not realize it yet, but Hashem has wired us to find our way back to Him. His way is straight and narrow, and as Scripture says, there is only one path. If you would like to explore this one path then ask God to reveal to you that one path.

If you would like to know Yeshua as your Messiah, then simply speak with God, saying:

> *Abba Father, if You are the One mankind has been searching for since creation and the only true way to connect with You is through Yeshua (Jesus), the Messiah of the Jewish people and the nations, then I would like to ask You to come into my heart so that You can reveal Yourself to me in spirit and truth. If You really are the way, then I want to know and follow You. Amen.*

To grow in your knowledge of God's Word and Yeshua's plan for your life, I encourage you to find a Bible-believing church or Messianic congregation. You can also find some resources about beginning your journey with Yeshua at my website, www.gesherinternational.com.

May God's peace be with you in the name of Yeshua.

GLOSSARY

Abba—Daddy

Adon Olam—the eternal Lord

Adonai—Most High God

Adonai-Nissi—God is my banner

Adonai Rofecha—the Lord your Healer

Adonai-Tzva'ot—Lord of Hosts

afikomen—the unleavened matzo that is broken in two during the early stages of the Passover Seder and set aside to be eaten after the meal as a dessert

amein—amen, so be it

Atarah—the embroidered neckband on the tallit that contains the blessing recited when a person puts the tallit on his shoulders.

Bamidbar—Numbers

bar mitzvah—Jewish ceremony that takes place when a boy reaches the age of thirteen to mark his acceptance of his religious duty and responsibility

Baruch Atah—"Blessed are You," a phrase often said at the beginning of Jewish prayers

basar echad—oneness, one flesh

bat mitzvah—Jewish ceremony that takes place when a girl reaches at least the age of twelve to mark her acceptance of her religious duty and responsibility.

Beelzebul—Satan

Ben Elohim—the Son of God

Bereishit—Genesis

bimah—a raised platform in a synagogue that contains the ark, the Torah, and the reading table used when chanting or reading portions of the Torah and the books of the Prophets

bitachon—trust

Bnei Yisrael—children of Israel

bris (also called a *brit milah*)—circumcision, performed eight days after a Jewish boy is born

B'rit Chadashah—New Testament

chen—favor

cheruv/cheruvim—cherub/cherubim, which are angelic beings

chesed—lovingkindness or grace

chillul Hashem—to desecrate the name of God

chuppah—canopy created by placing tallitot on poles; often used during Jewish weddings

dayenu—it is sufficient

d'rash—sermon

echad—one, especially the oneness of God the Father, God the Son, and God the Holy Spirit

El Elyon—God Most High

El Shaddai—God Almighty

Eloheinu—our God

emunah—faith

Erev Shavuot—the evening of Shavuot, which is the Feast of Weeks (see also Shavuot)

Etz Chayim—Tree of Life

Etz haDaat tov V'ra—Tree of the Knowledge of Good and Evil

Gan Eden—Garden of Eden

genizah—a section of a Jewish cemetery set aside for burying worn-out holy books, including the Torah, or documents containing the sacred name of God, YHVH or Adonai

gesher—*bridge*

gesher shalom—bridge of peace

goel—kinsman redeemer

Haftarah—a series of selections from the books of Nevi'im (the books of the Prophets) in the Old Testament (Tanakh) that are read publicly in Jewish congregations

halacha—the rabbinical way, or "the body of Jewish law supplementing the scriptural law and forming the legal part of the Talmud"[1]

HaMakom—the place

HaMashiach—*the Messiah*

Hamelech—King

hasatan—the devil

Hashem—God, the Name

Ivrit—a Hebrew or "boundary crosser"

kadima—forward

kal va-chomer—a logical course of deductive reasoning in talmudical hermeneutics that follows from simple to complex and/or from complex to simple

kanaph (or *kanaphecha*)—"wings," or tassels of the tallit

kavanah—Yiddish for "with intention from the bottom of one's heart"

kavod—the glory of God

kesher—Yiddish for connection

kippah—yarmulke, a small round cap worn by men to cover their heads

kishkes—Yiddish for "deep insides"

K'lal Yisrael—Yiddish for the "whole of Israel"

Kodesh HaKodashim—the Holy of Holies, the inner sanctuary of the ancient Jewish temple

kohanim—priests

kohen—priest

Kol Hashem—the voice of God

Kol Nidre—evening service on the eve of Yom Kippur (Day of Atonement)

Lech-Lecha—go or leave

Mashiach—Messiah

mikveh—ritual water immersion in Judaism

Mishikeinu—our Messiah

mishpocha—family

Mitzrayim—Egypt

mitzvot—commandments

mohel—person who performs a circumcision

Moshe Rabbeinu—Moses our Teacher

na'aseh v'nishma—do and obey

niddah—ritual state of being unclean as with the woman with the issue of blood in Mark 5:21–43

Pesach—Passover

Rabbeinu—our Teacher

Rabbi Shaul—Paul the apostle

Ruach Elohim—Spirit of God

Ruach HaKodesh—Holy Spirit

sandek—godfather, or one who has the role of holding the child on his lap during the blessings of circumcision

seder—a Jewish service and ceremonial dinner held the first night (or first two nights) of Passover

selah—a pause in time

Shabbat—the Jewish Sabbath, which begins at sundown on Friday and ends at sundown on Saturday

Shaddai—the Almighty

shalom—peace

shamash—one thread of the tzitzit that is longer than the other threads and is wound around the other threads and used to tie knots

Shavuot—the Feast of Weeks (also known as Pentecost), a Jewish holiday that takes place on the sixth day of the Hebrew month of Sivan, which falls between May 14 and June 15. It commemorates the important wheat harvest in Israel that was referenced in Exodus 34:22 and the anniversary of the day God gave the Torah to the entire nation of Israel assembled at Mount Sinai.

Shekinah—the presence of God

Shema—the oldest fixed daily prayer in Judaism, drawn from Deuteronomy 6:4–9; 11:13–21, and Numbers 15:37–41, which has been recited morning and night since ancient times

shlichim—apostles

shofar—a ram's-horn trumpet blown by the ancient Hebrews in battle and during religious observances and used in modern Judaism especially during Rosh Hashanah and at the end of Yom Kippur[2]

sukkah—shelter

tallit—Jewish prayer shawl; the plural form is tallitot

tallit gadol—large tallit

tallit katan—small tallit, often worn by men under their shirts with the tzitzit (tassels) left hanging out

talmidim—disciples

Tanakh—Old Testament

tefillin—phylacteries or Scripture boxes

tekhelet—a blue dye derived from a rare snail that was used for royal garments, in the tabernacle, and on the tassels of the tallit

Torah—first five books of the Old Testament, which were written by Moses

tza'arat—leprosy

tzitzit—fringes or tassels on the tallit

yachad—unity

yarmulke—a small round cap worn by men to cover their heads

yedid nefesh—beloved

Yeshua—Jesus

Yeshua HaMashiach—Jesus the Messiah

Yeshua Mishikeinu—Jesus our Messiah

Yeshua Rabbeinu—Jesus our Teacher

yetzer hara—the evil inclination

yetzer hatov—the good inclination

YHVH—the sacred name of God

Yoel haNavi—Joel the prophet

Yom Kippur—Day of Atonement, the holiest day in the Jewish year. All work is suspended and observers fast for twenty-five hours, beginning before sunset the evening before Yom Kippur and ending after nightfall on the day of Yom Kippur. It is a time when we "afflict the soul" and atone for sins committed and promises broken to God and between people.

NOTES

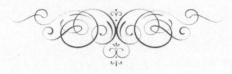

CHAPTER 1
THE MYSTERY
OF THE TALLIT

1. Merriam-Webster Online, s.v. "halacha," accessed July 21, 2016, http://merriam-webster.com/dictionary /halacha.

2. "The Tzitzit/Fringe," Tallit-Prayer Shawl, accessed May 20, 2016, http://www.tallit-prayershawl.com /articles-about-tallit/the-tzitzit-fringe/.

3. Ibid.

CHAPTER 2
HEARING GOD
UNDER THE TALLIT

1. Tiffany Ann Lewis, "Desperate for Jesus," Identity Network, accessed July 27, 2016, http://www.identity network.net/Articles-and-Prophetic-Words?blogid=20 93&view=post&articleid=76437&fldKeywords=&fld Author=&fldTopic=.

2. Although English Bibles typically include the Book of James, the accurate Hebrew name is *Jacob.* The name was corrupted as it passed from Hebrew to Greek to Latin to English, ultimately morphing into *James,* but in recent years there have been calls to restore the accurate name of the author of this book. For this

reason, throughout the book I use the name Jacob with James in brackets. For more information on this topic, please see Michael Brown, "Recovering the Lost Letter of Jacob," Charisma News, March 11, 2013, accessed May 20, 2016, http://www.charismanews .com/opinion/38591-recovering-the-lost-letter-of-jacob.

CHAPTER 3
THE PRESENCE AND COVERING OF GOD

1. Watchman Nee, *Spiritual Authority* (New York: Christian Fellowship Publishers, 1972), 10.

2. "Navigating the Bible: Deuteronomy Chapter 10," World ORT, accessed May 20, 2016, http://bible.ort .org/books/pentd2.asp?ACTION=displaypage&BOOK =5&CHAPTER=10.

CHAPTER 4
YESHUA AND THE TALLIT:
HEALING IN HIS WINGS

1. Alfred J. Kotlatch, *The Second Jewish Book of Why* (Middle Village, NY: Jonathan David Publishers, 1988), 70.

CHAPTER 5
MYTHS AND MISCONCEPTIONS
ABOUT THE TALLIT

1. Philip Birnbaum, *Encyclopedia of Jewish Concepts* (Brooklyn, NY: Hebrew Publishing Company, 1975), 244.

CHAPTER 6
A JOURNEY OF FAITH
UNDER THE TALLIT

1. *Ushpizin*, dir. Gidi Dar (Jerusalem, Israel: Gidi Dar and Rafi Bukai, 2004).

2. Rebecca Greenwood, "2010: A Year to Rise to New Levels of Faith," The Elijah List, December 29, 2009, accessed July 27, 2016, http://www.elijahlist.com /words/display_word/8341.

CHAPTER 7
THE TALLIT AS A BRIDGE

1. "Gesher Tzar Me'od—The World Is a Narrow Bridge," ReformJudaism.org, accessed May 20, 2016, http:// www.reformjudaism.org/practice/prayers-blessings /gesher-tzar-meod-world-narrow-bridge.

2. Chuck Missler, "A Hidden Message: The Gospel in Genesis," Koinonia House, accessed May 3, 2016, http://www.khouse.org/articles/1996/44/.

CHAPTER 8
THE TALLIT AND
THE LAST DAYS

1. Joshua Muravchik, "How the UN Was Perverted into a Weapon against Israel," *New York Post*, July 26, 2014, accessed May 25, 2016, http://nypost.com /2014/07/26/how-the-united-nations-was-perverted -into-a-weapon-against-israel/.

2. Sarah Pulliam Bailey, "American Evangelicals' Support for Israel Is Waning, Reports Say," Religion News Service via *The Huffington Post*, April 9, 2014, accessed May 25, 2016, 2014, http://www .huffingtonpost.com/2014/04/09/american-evanglicals -israel_n_5118417.html.

3. Elise Labott, "John Kerry: Some Sanctions Relief Money for Iran Will Go to Terrorism," CNN, January 21, 2016, accessed May 25, 2016, http://www.cnn.com /2016/01/21/politics/john-kerry-money-iran-sanctions -terrorism.

4. Chas Danner, "Report: ISIS Has Recruited as Many as 30,000 Foreigners in the Past Year," *New York* magazine, accessed May 25, 2016, http://nymag.com /daily/intelligencer/2015/09/isis-has-recruited-as -many-as-30000-foreigners.html.

5. Matt Slick, "Examples of Persecution of People Who Do Not Agree with Homosexuality," Christian Apologetics and Research Ministry, accessed May 25, 2016, https://carm.org/homosexual-persecution-of -christians.

6. Francis Frangipane, "The Real Jesus Is Calling Us to Do the Impossible in the Middle of the Storm," The Elijah List, April 26, 2007, accessed July 27, 2016, http://www.elijahlist.com/words/display_word/5226.

7. Ibid.

GLOSSARY

1. Merriam-Webster Online, s.v. "halacha."

2. Merriam-Webster Online, s.v. "shofar," accessed July 21, 2016, http://merriam-webster.com/dictionary /shofar.

CONNECT WITH US!

CHARISMA HOUSE

(Spiritual Growth)

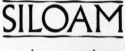

SILOAM

(Health)

REALMS

(Fiction)